Daily Dose of Dependence on God

Daily Devotional for Women: Are You in a Storm?
Seek God's Sunshine to Bring You Through

PRISCILLA CALCOTE

WestBow Press books may be ordered through booksellers or by contacting:

WestBow Press
A Division of Thomas Nelson & Zondervan
1663 Liberty Drive
Bloomington, IN 47403
www.westbowpress.com
1 (866) 928-1240

ISBN: 978-1-4908-4372-8 (sc)
ISBN: 978-1-4908-4373-5 (e)

Library of Congress Control Number: 2014912160

Print information available on the last page.

WestBow Press rev. date: 2/25/2015

To all the women who are in pain and who rely on others to bring them out of their storms. In 2011, God spoke to me, and I listened. God told me to stop being a rescuer (trying to fix everyone's problems). He also told me to stop depending on earthly man to resolve my problems. He said, "Let go, and depend on Me." After much praying and fasting, I knew that my storms were preparing me for a greater calling. In order for God's purpose to come forth, I had to recognize that my storms were not about me but about my obedience to God's will. God instructed me to become His disciple and profess God's faithfulness through testimony and His Word.

Foreword

When Priscilla shared with me that she was inspired by God to write this book, I was a bit surprised—not because I didn't think she was capable but by the fact that she decided to take such a leap of faith by taking on such a huge task that I know was out of her comfort zone. She has shared with me some of the personal struggles she had been dealing with, and I know writing a book was the last thing she was planning to do. Needless to say, I am so happy and personally inspired that she answered God's call and just said yes to His will and to His purpose for her at this point and time. I have since seen how God has equipped her for this assignment and helped her to find all of the necessary resources to make this happen; all the while she continues to totally depend on God to lead her and guide her each and every step of the way. Her book *Daily Dose of Dependence on God* is a perfect title that reflects her personal journey. It provides examples of how her faith was key to overcoming all of the obstacles that have been thrown at her over the past few years.

At the beginning of Priscilla's journey, I saw that she was broken both naturally and spiritually. She was becoming overwhelmed by her circumstances, but over time, I have witnessed God's amazing sustaining power and have seen how He has positively intervened in every aspect of her life—all because she dared to trust and depend on Him and Him alone. Hence, she has since transformed into a spiritually enlightened, empowered, and peaceful soul. She has demonstrated to me that God never fails and that His grace and His mercy far exceed all of our expectations if we choose to trust and depend on Him. I am so fortunate to have her as a dear friend and to call her my sister in Christ.

I pray that by reading this book, you will share in her victory and develop your own personal testimony by establishing your own daily dependence on God. I know I have.

Glory Franklin

Preface

God predestined the existence of this book before I was even a thought in my parents' minds. God's love for me and other women is so great that He persistently called me for His purpose. One day I could not rely on earthly man or things anymore to rescue me from the storms of this world. During my adult life, many women, in vast numbers, would express to me their incredibly heartrending circumstances, such as medical issues, domestic abuse, sexual abuse, sibling conflict, parent conflict, children difficulties, drug/alcohol abuse, job difficulties, and job loss. I cried out to God in 2011 and said, "Lord, why are they sharing their lives with me? I am having my own challenges, and I am too weak to help anyone. I am also ashamed to say I am not depending on You for all."

Then the Lord said to me, "Why not you? When are you going to start solely depending on Me? Have I not kept you when you wanted to give up?" The purpose of this daily devotional is to empower women through God's Word and profession of God's faithfulness so women can begin to trust and depend on God in all things!

Acknowledgments

First, I would like to give praise and honor to the almighty God for His unconditional love and favor in my life. If God had not loved me and wanted me to have a closer walk with Him, where would I be today? God's love for me allowed me to step out on faith and trust Him and Him only! Faith moves God, and that is why this book is now published.

Secondly, I would like to acknowledge my daughter, who had the idea for the book cover design. My daughter Chloe is the angel that I prayed for fifteen years ago. She is not only beautiful but also outspoken, confident, and definitely a daughter of God. She has a warm heart and believes in equality for all. Chloe believes and knows there is only one true God, who never fails.

Thirdly, I would like to acknowledge my nephew, Demetri, who designed the cover of this book. Demetri not only is an artist but also has a heart of gold that is missing among so many. Demetri's heart exemplifies characteristics of Christ.

Last, but not least, I would like to acknowledge my "earthly angels," my mom and dad, who celebrated fifty years of marriage on August 15, 2014. My parents' hearts are solid gold. They have never failed me. They are the ultimate parents. I thank God for allowing me to be their daughter—again, another act of God's love for me.

Introduction

Dependence is not a hindrance if it's on *God*.

Dependence:
I can do all things through Christ which strengthened me.
—Philippians 4:13

Trust:
when she had heard of Jesus, came in the press behind, and touched his garment. For she said, if I may touch but his clothes, I shall be whole. And straightway the fountain of blood was dried up: and she felt in her body that she was healed of that plague.
—Mark 5:27–29

Unconditional love:
and stood at his feet behind Him weeping, and began to wash his feet with tears and did wipe them with the hairs of her head, and kissed his feet, and anointed with the ointment.
—Luke 7:38

Forgiveness:
When Jesus lifted up himself, and saw none but the woman, he said, unto her, Woman, where are those thine accusers? hath no man condemned thee? She said, No man Lord, and Jesus said unto her, neither do I condemn thee, go and sin no more.
—John 8:10–11

Prologue

My personal testimonies:

1) Even though God gave me free will, many times in the past, I followed my own will or the will of others. But God did not abandon me, judge me, or stop loving me. Instead, my God forgave me and showed me unbelievable favor when I began to trust and depend on Him with my life.

2) I now realize that forgiving someone does not need validation by that person. Jesus, who died on the cross for me, and new mercies daily from God provide validation.

3) A humbled spirit is a delivered spirit.

4) A "perfect love" comes from God and only God. God loves me unconditionally. God cradles my mind when I become stressed, carries me when I am weary, forgives me when I am too much to handle, holds my hand, and directs my path. My God has never let my hand go. I shall never let His unchanging hand and loving heart go either—not ever.

5) When I focus on the given day, my God gives me peace. I will not fret over tomorrow because I believe my God has already gone before me and worked out all situations that may arise that are trying to defeat me from being a vessel for God.

6) Finally feeling whole and not seeking others to define or complete me. Knowing that only God can fulfill my life.

7) Not being conformed to the image of what others think I should be but trusting God in His plans for my life.

8) Lacking nothing because I have God, who fills me from head to toe.

9) Awakening to a new day with the presence of the Lord embracing me!

10) By remaining focused on God, I found spiritual peace and satisfaction while being physically alone in all situations, even when the situation was a time where couples, families, and friends gathered. I was not lonely but peaceful in the presence of God.

JANUARY

Dose of God's

PEACE

January 1

It is of the Lord's mercies that we are not consumed, because His compassions fail not.
—**Lamentations 3:22–23**

***L*adies,**
It is a new year and a new day! Last year's trials are now this year's triumps, because our Savior, Jesus Christ, has brought us out of the past into the light of a new year. So move forward with joy in your heart, because God is the faithful one.

January 2

Forget the former things; do not dwell on the past. See, I am doing a new thing! Now it springs up; do you not perceive it? I am making a way in the wilderness and streams in the wasteland.
—**Isaiah 43:18–19**

***L*adies,**
Whatever you endured last year, it is done. Do not look back or anxiously worry about tomorrow. Hold the unchanging hand of God, and allow Him to lead you. In the midst of your journey, God will provide all you need. Trust and depend only on Him.

January 3

Be anxious for nothing, but in everything by prayer and supplication with thanksgiving let your requests be made known to God. And the *Peace of God,* which *surpasses* all comprehension, shall *Guard* your heart and minds in Christ Jesus.
—**Philippians 4:6–7**

***L*adies,**
The Scripture says be anxious for nothing, so in this year, pray, pray, pray, and the peace of God shall cradle your mind and your heart in all circumstances. Trust and depend on God.

January 4

And be not conformed to this world: but be ye transformed by the renewing of your mind, that ye may prove what is that good, and acceptable, and perfect, will of God's.
—**Romans 12:2**

***L*adies,**
God has the perfect plan for you this year, but you cannot worry about what others think about you. Yes, they will see a change in you, and yes, they will comment, but remember, that is the trick of the Devil. The Devil will slither his way into the minds of those you love to try to put a roadblock in your way. Continue to trust and depend on God. As my pastor says every Sunday, "No one on this earth has a heaven or hell to put you into but God!" Be blessed!

January 5

But in a great house there are not only vessels of gold and silver, but also of wood and of earth; and some to honor, and some to dishonor. If a man therefore purges himself from these, he shall be a vessel unto honor, sanctified, and meet for the master's use and prepared unto every good work. Flee also youthful lusts: but follow righteousness faith, charity and peace, with them that call on the Lord out of a pure heart. But foolish and unlearned questions avoid, knowing that they do gender strifes And the servant of the Lord must not strive; but be gentle unto all men apt to teach, patient; in meekness instructing those that oppose themselves, if God peradventure will give them repentance to the acknowledging of the truth. And that they may recover themselves out of the snare of the devil, who are taken captive by him at his will.
—**2 Timothy 2:20–26**

***L*adies,**
Is God calling you to testify how He is sustaining or has brought you through your pain from last year? Do the work of God. Become that vessel. Only God's strength can help you empower another woman in pain. Avoid the naysayers, and continue to walk in God's purpose, not man's purpose, which has no salvation. Go spread the good news.

January 6

Wherein ye greatly rejoice, though now for a season, if need be, ye are in heaviness through manifold temptations: That the trial of your faith, being much more precious than of gold that perisheth, though it be tried with fire, might be found unto praise and honor and glory at the appearing of *Jesus Christ.*
—**1 Peter 1:6–7**

***L*adies,**
Do not faint in the midst of these trials; they're just proof that your faith is genuine. God has a plan for you to continue on your journey that will result in praise and glory and honor when our Lord is revealed.

January 7

And they came to Him, and awoke Him, saying, Master, Master, we perish. Then He arose, and rebuked the wind and the raging of the water: and they ceased, and there was a calm.
—**Luke 8:24**

***L*adies,**
Remember Jesus can and will calm any storm. Trust and depend on Him as you journey through this week. He is faithful!

January 8

Be *Strong* and of a good *Courage, Fear not,* nor be afraid of them: for the Lord thy God, He it is that doth go with thee; he will *not fail* thee, nor *forsake* thee.
—**Deuteronomy 31:6**

***L*adies,**
Let us pray: Lord, teach us to have faith, because with faith there is no fear. God, You said You will not fail, judge, or abandon us. Guide us to follow Your plans for us this year. Almighty God, anoint every step we make each day this year. When

we approach naysayers, let Your Word trample their unbelief. In Jesus' name we pray, amen!

January 9

If we confess ours sins, and just to *forgive* us our sins and to cleanse us from all unrighteousness.
—**1 John 1:9**

***L*adies,**
Our God is forgiving. Do not allow the convictions of others or of yourselves stop you from moving into your blessing. Jesus loves you, and He offers unconditional love. Ask for forgiveness and it shall be given. Be blessed!

January 10

Blessed be God, even the Father of our Lord Jesus Christ, the Father of Mercies and the God of all comfort who comforteth us in All our tribulation, that we may be able to comfort them which are in any trouble, by the comfort wherewith we ourselves are comforted of God.
—**2 Corinthians 1:3–4**

***L*adies,**
I want to share what God confirmed to me as my pastor spoke in Bible study last night. Even though we may be going through our own trials, we must do as Paul did and comfort others and depend on God. The Bible message stated the things we need to have a happy new year:

1) Bless God (worship Him daily). God is so worthy!
2) Praise God in times of trouble.
3) Remember Jesus is the Savior, and God is the Father of salvation.
4) God's mercy gives us a second chance; God is so faithful to us.
5) No matter what tribulation (pressure, trial, problem, or persecution) comes our way, this year, God will comfort us.

As God comforts you in your trials, be a comforter for another. Be blessed!

January 11

For as he thinketh in his heart so is he.
—**Proverbs 23:7**

Death and Life are in the power of the tongue: and they that love it shall eat the fruit thereof.
—**Proverbs 18:21**

***L*adies,**
Proclaim, declare, and speak joy unto yourselves for this year. No more pity parties; it's celebration time! Our God is faithful. Let's rewind. If you had pain, depression, illness, or a broken heart last year but God kept you from losing your mind, and if you can say, "Yes, God did," then it is time to celebrate the goodness of our God!

January 12

But Thanks be to God, which Giveth us the Victory through our Lord Jesus Christ.
—**1 Corinthians 15:57**

***L*adies,**
Trust God. He will bring glory after all you endured. He will bring victory; seek, ask, and knock. Your blessings are within your reach!

January 13

And let the Peace of God rule in your heart, to the which also ye are called in one body; and be ye thankful. Let the Word of Christ dwell in you richly in all wisdom; teaching and admonishing one another in psalms and hymns and spiritual songs, singing with grace in your hearts to the Lord. And whatsoever ye do in word or

deed do all in the name of The Lord Jesus, giving thanks to God and the father by Him.
—**Colossians 3:15–17**

***L*adies,**
God is so worthy of our praise. For any mountain that appears unmovable, the key to getting around it is praising, singing to, and glorifying God. He will provide insurmountable peace as you move into your blessing.

January 14

The spirit of the Lord God is upon me; because the Lord hath anointed me to preach good tidings unto the meek; he hath sent me to bind up the brokenhearted, to proclaim liberty to the captives, and the opening of the prison to them that are bound;
—**Isaiah 61:1**

***L*adies,**
Are you brokenhearted—soul sick and spiritually depressed by the world, circumstances, and people around you? Are you trying to find fulfillment in other people and or things? Are you spiritually bound and blind?

Good news: depend on Jesus. Jesus is the only healer of a broken heart! Jesus' light restores spiritual sight, which will guide you out of your storm into freedom.

January 15

For do I now persuade men or God? or do I seek to please men? For if I yet pleased men, I should not be the servant of Christ.
—**Galatians 1:10**

***L*adies,**
Are you trying to win the approval of others (boss, friend, family, or spouse)? If so, why?

Do they unconditionally:

- Love you despite your faults?
- Understand you at all times, even during your most difficult moments?
- Rescue you in the nick of time?
- Listen to you in the midnight hour?
- Comfort you when you are hurting?
- Provide for you when you are financially burdened?

God has and will continue to do these things if you trust and serve Him.

January 16

Thou wilt keep HER in perfect peace, whose mind is stayed on thee: because she trusteth in thee. Trust ye in the Lord forever; for in the Lord Jehovah is Everlasting strength.
—**Isaiah 26:3–4**

***L*adies,**
Are the winds roaring in your life? Winds: questionable job security, depleted savings, unrealistic children, unloving spouses/boyfriends, fair-weather friends, and haters.
Are you losing sight of Jesus and taking circumstances in your own hands? Perfect peace comes from God when your mind remains on Him by praying and reading His Word daily!

January 17

Thou shalt not be afraid for the terror by night, nor by the arrow that flieth by day; Nor for the pestilence that walketh in darkness; nor for the destruction that wasteth at noonday.
—**Psalm 91:5–6**

There shall no evil befall her, neither shall any plague come nigh her dwelling. For HE shall give His angels charge over her, to keep her in all thy ways.
—**Psalm 91:10–11**

***L*adies,**
Do you fear the uncertainty of our world today? Are you allowing Satan, the tempter, to have you doubt the Word of God as Eve did? Well, acknowledge that your fears are too strong for you to handle, and place them in God's capable hands. Trust Him!

January 18

My soul, wait silently for God alone, for my expectation is from Him.
—**Psalm 62:5**

***L*adies,**
Whatever you are waiting for from God, wait patiently and expectantly. Trust Him; He will deliver!

January 19

Now the Lord of himself give you peace always by all means. The Lord be with you all.
—**2 Thessalonians 3:16**

***L*adies,**
Our God has what you need: peace. Be still, see the gift of today, and rejoice in it. Rejoice in the simple things in life: laughing with your children, holding hands with a loved one, watching your favorite sitcoms all day, sharing a dinner with a good friend, spending the day with your aging parents.
Tomorrow is not promised; find peace today! Trust God; He will deliver the peace you need.

January 20

God is no respecter of persons
—**<u>Acts 10:34</u>**

***L*adies,**
God does not play favoritism. He loves us equally. So, when your sister is being blessed, do not hate on her. Instead, be excited for her. Your blessing is on its way. Ladies, we have allowed Satan to turn us against each other (cheating with another woman's husband, lying to the boss in an attempt to steal her position at work, secretly hoping another woman's children fail, and the list goes on). Let's prove to the world that we are Christian sisters, not a reality-show train wreck!

January 21

For it is God's will that by doing good you should silence the ignorant talk of foolish men. Live as free men, but do not use your freedom as a cover up for evil; live as servants of God.
—**<u>1 Peter 2:15–16</u>**

The speech, "I've Been to the Mountaintop" of Martin Luther King said it best, "Follow God's will and do not worry about anything or fear any man."

January 22

Enter into His gates with Thanksgiving and into His courts with Praise. Be Thankful unto Him, and Bless His Name.
—**<u>Psalm 100:4</u>**

***L*adies,**
Are you grateful for all that God has provided for you thus far?
Ingratitude (being ungrateful) will make you vulnerable to Satan's attack.

For God knows that when you eat of it your eyes will be opened, and you will be like God, knowing good and evil.
—**Genesis 3:5**

***L*adies,**
Are you being lured by the lie that something else or someone else is better? Stay focused on God's Word. It shall not fail you but instead empower you to sustain against all of Satan's schemes and allies.

January 23

Be Joyful in hope,
Patient in affliction, Faithful in prayer.
—**Romans 12:12**

***L*adies,**
This year has blessings awaiting you. Trust God to deliver.
Live each day with joy in anticipation. Daily prayer will build your faith so much that you will be amazed at how patient you have become, even in the midst of the storm.

January 24

Do not be misled: Bad company corrupts good character.
—**1 Corinthians 15:33**

***L*adies,**
Are you entertaining bad company by gossiping, cheating, feeling sorry for yourself, consuming unhealthy foods, and hating on others who trust God? If so, stop and pray for deliverance.

January 25

Bless the Lord, Oh my soul, and forget not all His benefits; Who forgiveth all thine iniquities; who healeth all thy diseases. Who redeemeth thy life from destruction who crowneth thee with loving kindness and tender mercies.
—**Psalm 103:2–4**

Guilt is seeing what you have done (not forgiving, gossiping, cheating, being dishonest).
Shame is seeing yourself as a failure (being infertile, divorced, abandoned, a victim of abuse, a teen mom, an ex-addict).
Guilt looks at the sin; shame looks at you.

Jesus sacrificed His life, which forgave the guilt, and His blood covered the shame.

***L*adies,** leave your past with God. He has already forgiven you! Move forward into a year of blessing from God for you.

January 26

Thus saith the Lord; Cursed be the man that trusteth in man, and maketh flesh his arm and whose heart departeth from the Lord.
—**Jeremiah 17:5**

Cast thy burden upon the Lord, and He shall sustain thee: he shall never suffer the righteous to be moved.
—**Psalm 55:22**

***L*adies,**
Are you trusting God and not the world?

January 27

2 Corinthians 5:17
"Therefore if anyone is in Christ, she is a new creation. The old passed away, behold the new shall come."

***L*adies,**
This is the last week of the first month of this new year. Have you moved closer to God's radiant light? Have you experienced peace since letting go of some people and circumstances from last year? If the answer is yes, continue your walk with Christ. If the answer is no, seek Jesus.

January 28

I have been crucified with Christ; and it is no longer I that live, but Christ living in me: and that life which I now live in the flesh I live in faith, the faith which is in the Son of God, who loved me, and gave himself up for me.
—**Galatians 2:20**

***L*adies,**
Are you walking and talking different this year?
Is the new you because of Jesus walking in front as a guide, alongside as a support, and behind as a protector?

January 29

As a dog that returneth to his vomit, so is a fool that repeateth her folly.
—**Proverbs 26:11**

But as for you, ye thought evil against me; but God meant it unto good, to bring pass, as it is this day, to save much people alive.
—**Genesis 50:20**

I am Alpha and Omega the beginning and the ending, saith the Lord, which is and which is to come, the Almighty.
—**Revelation 1:8**

***L*adies,**
Are you turning back to your old ways from the past? Stop and remember God saved you from the wicked ways of Satan! God is in control; He shall not fail you.

January 30

You turned my wailing into dancing; you removed my sackcloth and clothed me with joy, that my heart may sing your praises and not be silent. Lord my God, I will praise you forever.
—**Psalm 30:11–12**

***L*adies,**
God has been so faithful to us that we must praise Him. We are still here despite our selfish ways. Praise God now and forever

January 31

And the man said, The woman whom thou gavest to be with me, she gave me of the tree, and I did eat. And the Lord God unto the woman, What is this that thou hast done? And the woman said, The serpent beguiled me, and I did eat.
—**Genesis 3:12–13**

***L*adies,**
Do not feel guilty about your past mistakes; God forgives all.

FEBRUARY

Dose of God's

LOVE

February 1

Give Thanks to the Lord, for He is good; His Love endures forever.
—**1 Chronicles 16:34**

***L*adies,**
Do you want a love that is undying, unconditional, and trustworthy? Trust and depend on God, and witness His love and new mercies each day.

February 2

For God so Loved the world, that He gave His only begotten Son, that whosoever believeth on him should not perish, but have eternal life.
—**John 3:16**

***L*adies,**
Trust in the Love that God has to offer; there is none like it.

February 3

I will be glad and rejoice in your love, for you saw my affliction and knew the anguish of my soul.
—**Psalm 31:7**

***L*adies,**
Praise God for carrying you through. Only God's enduring love delivers.

February 4

Do not withhold your mercy from me, O'Lord; may your love and your truth always protect me.
—**Psalm 40:11**

Ladies,
God knows we are weak, and that is why He gives us another chance (mercy). He provides unconditional love and directs us from our sinful ways. That's love ... God's Love.

February 5

That Christ may dwell in your hearts by faith; that ye, being rooted and grounded in love, may be able to comprehend with all saints what is the breadth, and length, and depth and height; And to know the love of Christ, which passeth knowledge, that ye might be filled with all the fullness of God.
—**Ephesians 3:17–19**

Ladies,
If you have faith and obtain a close personal relationship with God, you will experience a love greater than you have ever known.

- A love that never fails regardless of your faults
- A love that comforts a weary body
- A love that cradles a restless mind
- A love that provides in a time of need
- A love that always loves

February 6

My Little Children, let us not love in word or talk but indeed and in truth.
—**1 John 3:18**

Ladies,
Are you receiving or giving love in word only? If so, when it is pronounced, it will cease. But if the love you are receiving or giving is demonstrated in deed, the acts shall exemplify love that is sincere and real. The greatest deed of all is Christ's crucifixion that saved us all. Now *that* is love.

February 7

But when the kindness and love of God our Savior appeared, He saved us not because of righteous things we had done, but because of His mercy. He saved us through the washing of rebirth and renewal by the Holy Spirit.
—**Titus 3:4–7**

***L*adies,**
Thank God for His love and kindness, which delivers mercy and provides an easier route for sinners like you and me.

February 8

I have loved you with an everlasting love.
—**Jeremiah 31:3**

***L*adies,**
God's love is forever. His love endures, even through the storms of life. He never gives up on us. Nothing we do can end the love of God.

February 9

Love never Fails
—**1 Corinthians 13:8**

Excerpt from John W. Martens article "Love Never Fails":

> Love never fails because God, who is love, never fails. Human Love can be disordered and disintegrate because they can be built upon our own misguided hopes and desires. We mistake what we want or how we perceive something for how things must be or truly are. When Jesus spoke in the synagogue in Nazareth, his initial proclamation was greeted warmly: "All spoke highly of him and were amazed at the gracious words that came from his mouth." Yet when Jesus speaks

of God's healing love among the gentiles, drawing on examples from the prophets and Elijah and Elisha, Luke presents a group of people suddenly enraged. How could things change so fast? Luke does not offer us many details, but it seems people's expectations regarding God's salvation were not met. Jesus had just spoken of his prophetic fulfillment in the synagogue, so why would he place God's fulfillment of Israel's hopes among the gentiles? In addition, something else is bubbling under the surface with respect to Jesus, as to whether he is truly the one. After all "Isn't this the son of Joseph?"

We think we know how things ought to go, and we are often certain we know who people are. We are quick to order the world according to our own wishes and desires. Because of this, the proclamation of the word of God does not always fall on fertile soil. It is not what we wanted, hoped for or expected. It is too challenging, too generous or too different. The person God has chosen for a task is not someone who we feel has the qualifications.

***L*adies,**
God qualifies you, not man.

February 10

But God, being rich in mercy, because of the great love with which He loved us, even when we were dead in our trespasses, made us alive together with Christ ... by grace you have been saved.
—**Ephesians 2:4–5**

***L*adies,**
The bondage is over. God has forgiven our trespasses and delivered us! Things of the past (abuse, rejection, addiction, adultery, bitterness, depression, illness, loneliness, promiscuity, envy, anger, shame from abortion, shame from divorce, pain of miscarriage, and pain of being infertile) are no more!

February 11

For we are God's handiwork, created in Christ Jesus to do good works, which God prepared in advance for us to do.
—**Ephesians 2:10**

***L*adies,**
God loves you. Others may make you feel you are not talented, not attractive, or not smart enough. People may disappoint you, reject you, and even wound your spirit. If you learn to receive your value from God, who says you are amazing, beautiful, and one of a kind, you will begin to feel accepted, approved, forgiven, and confident. Allow God to be first in your life.

February 12–13

I will sing of the Lord's great love forever; with my mouth I will make your faithfulness known through all generations.
—**Psalm 89:1**

***L*adies**
Do not be silent this year! Testify to others on how God has saved you, has healed you, has forgiven you, has provided for you, has loved you, has protected you, and has delivered you!

February 14–15

Love is patient, love is kind, It does not envy, it does not boast, it is not rude, it is not self-seeking, it is not easily angered, it keeps no record of wrongs. Love does not delight in evil but rejoices with the truth. It always protects, always trusts, always hopes, always perseveres. Love never fails. But where there are prophecies, they will cease; where there are tongues, they will be stilled; where there is knowledge it will pass away.
—**1 Corinthians 13:4–8**

***L*adies,**
Stop looking for perfect love in the world we live in. Only Jesus can love you like no other.

February 16

And the God of all grace, who called you to his eternal glory in Christ, after you have suffered a little while, will himself restore you and make you strong, firm and steadfast
—1 Peter 5:10

***L*adies,**
Are you surviving or thriving? God loves you so much that He has brought you out of last year and its trials. If you have the attitude, "Well, I survived," stop it. You must not keep that survival mentality. God has doors of blessings waiting for you to open. He wants the next part of your life to be better than the first. But you have to trust and depend on God to provide you with His favor.

February 17

My grace is sufficient for thee; for my strength is made perfect in weakness. Therefore I will boast all the more gladly about my weakness, so that Christ's power may rest on me.
—2 Corinthians 12:9

***L*adies,**
God truly loves you. When you become weak due to life circumstances, put your faith in God. He will strengthen you beyond what you ever expected. God will shield you with a calm spirit so you may endure anything!

February 18

Let us therefore come boldly unto the throne of grace, that we may obtain mercy, and find grace to help in time of need.
—**Hebrews 4:16**

***L*adies,**
Drop to the feet of Christ, and ask for His help. Then watch His miracles come forth in your lives.

February 19

I can do all things through Christ who strengthens me.
—**Philippians 4:13**

***L*adies,**
Nothing is impossible for God. Ask, seek, and knock, and it shall be done in Jesus' name. Have faith and believe it is going to happen, regardless of how the situation appears. When your blessing unfolds, give the almighty God praise.

February 20

When they kept on questioning him, he straightened up and said to them "Let any one of you who is without sin be the first to throw a stone at her."
—**John 8:7**

***L*adies,**
How many times have you been accused by those you thought had your back? Who accused you without examining the entire situation? Who accused you of a mistake that you had no control over? Who accused you without admitting fault in the situation? Who accused you of being indecisive? Who accused you to make himself or herself look better?

Listen … stop stressing over your accuser's insecurities; instead, praise our God for sending a forgiver who leaves us with peace of mind.

February 21

Give us this day our daily bread
—**Matthew 6:11**

Therefore do not worry about tomorrow, for tomorrow will worry about itself.
—**Matthew 6:34**

***L*adies,**
Are you guilty of asking God for future blessings? According to the Lord's Prayer, we are to ask God for what we need that day only. We are not to fret about the future. If we fret, we are not trusting God to make a way. Do not forget how God brought you through a situation in the past that you did not think you could make it through. Each day is a gift to cherish before it is gone forever.

February 22

Do you not know that your body is a temple of the Holy Spirit, who is in you, whom you have received from God? You are not your own.
—**1 Corinthians 6:19**

***L*adies,**
You are a holy temple of God, and until you become married, your body is not for sharing. "Well," you may be thinking, "I did share it outside of wedlock or even in wedlock with someone other than my husband." Will God cast you out? No! John 8:11 states, "she said, No man, Lord. And Jesus said unto her, neither do I condemn thee: go, and sin no more."

February 23

Let each of you look not only to his own interests, but also to the interests of others.
—**Philippians 2:4**

No one should seek their own good, but the good of others.
—**1 Corinthians 10:24**

People will be lovers of themselves, lovers of money, boastful, proud, abusive, disobedient to their parents, ungrateful, unholy, without love, unforgiving, slanderous, without self-control, brutal, not lovers of the good, treacherous, rash, and conceited, lovers of pleasure rather than lovers of God ... having a form of godliness but denying its power. Have nothing to do with such people.
—**2 Timothy 3:2–5**

February 24

He heals the brokenhearted and binds up their wounds.
—**Psalm 147:3**

***L*adies,**
God can do anything. Nothing is impossible. Faith and trust in God almighty can heal a physical wound or an emotional, painful, irritating, and lingering wound.

February 25

For if you forgive others their trespasses, your heavenly Father will also forgive you.
—**Matthew 6:14**

***L*adies,**
To have God answer your prayers, you must first forgive all those who mistreated you. Forgive them; your blessings are too precious to miss over forgiveness! It does not matter if the person refuses to accept your apology; God will release you from that situation and answer your prayers. Never allow anyone to block what God has for you.

February 26

And we know that in All things God works for the good of those who love him, who have been called according to His purpose.
—**Romans 8:28**

***L*adies,**
At the end of your storm, God's sunlight will reveal His purpose.

February 27

Be alert and sober mind. Your enemy the devil prowls around like a roaring lion looking for someone to devour.
—**1 Peter 5:8**

***L*adies,**
Stay alert at all times! Satan can visit you in any form to steer you off the path of God's will for your future.

February 28 and 29

Jesus immediately reached out his hand took hold of her, saying to her, "Oh you of little faith, why did you doubt?
—**Matthew 14:31**

***L*adies,**
Stop doubting. Give God praise and honor. Look at what God has done for you. He has brought you through another month in this new year. Continue to hold His unchanging hand as He leads you through March.

MARCH

Dose of

FOCUSING ON GOD

March 1

Father, Forgive Them, They know not what they do.
—**Luke 23:24**

***L*adies,**
According to Dictionary.com, the definition of a father is a person who originated or established something. He is someone who exercises paternal care over other people. A father protects and is a provider.
On the cross, Jesus called on God by saying, "Father," because Jesus knew God as the originator of all things. Jesus called on His Father because Jesus knew He was the only protector of all men and provided mercy to the fallen, forgiving them of their sins.

***L*adies,**
Your Father will protect, provide for, and forgive you.

March 2

He saved us, not because of righteous things we had done, but because of his mercy.
—**Titus 3:5**

***L*adies,**
God's mercy is endless …

March 3

David said to Gad, "I am in deep distress. Let us fall into the hands of the Lord, for his mercy is great; but do not let me fall into human hands.
—**2 Samuel 24:14**

***L*adies,**
God's mercy cannot be depleted, only man's mercy. Your family and friends will get tired of giving you a second and third chance, but God will love you until the end. God's mercy is always connected to forgiveness.

March 4

Return, faithless Israel; declares the Lord, "I will frown on you no longer, for I am faithful, declares the Lord, I will not be angry forever. Only acknowledge your guilt you have rebelled against the Lord your God, you have scattered your favors to foreign gods under every spreading tree, and have not obeyed me, declares the Lord.
—**Jeremiah 3:12–13**

***L*adies,**
God offers forgiveness, but we must acknowledge our wrongdoings. God is faithful. He forgives.

March 5

Today shall thou be with me in paradise.
Jesus hung on the cross he was between two criminals. The first criminal's heart was hardened and could not "see" and "doubted" the Power of Jesus.
The second criminal "owned" that he deserved the crucifixion. He did not blame others for his current situation. He knew he was not worthy but repented and asked Jesus to forgive him so that he may have everlasting life in heaven.
—**Luke 23:43**

***L*adies,**
Stop blaming others for your current situation; instead, take ownership of your sins and God will forgive you.

March 6

Today thou shall be with me in paradise.
—**Luke 23:43**

***L*adies,**
Jesus is gracious; His grace toward us has set us free from sin and death!
Praise God!

March 7

Today thou shall be with me in paradise
—**Luke 23:43**

***L*adies,**
Do not harden your heart; offer grace and mercy toward others. Even while Jesus suffered on the cross, he had compassion and offered everlasting life in God's kingdom to the repentant criminal.

March 8

Woman, behold thy son … behold thy mother
—**John 19:26–27**

***L*adies,**
In Jesus' final moments on the cross, He showed love to Mary by securing her future. Jesus told John, His disciple, to watch over her as if she were his own mother. Are you taking care of your parents while they are still alive? Do you call and visit frequently, making sure they are okay?

March 9

Honor your father and mother, so that you may live long in the land that the Lord your God is giving you.
—**Exodus 20:12**

***L*adies,**
In order to receive the blessings God has purposed in your life, you must honor your parents.

Honoring: call, visit, spend quality time, and respect them.

March 10

Jesus said unto him, Thou shalt love the Lord thy God with all thy heart, and with all thy soul, and with thy entire mind. This is the first and great commandment.
—**Matthew 22:37–38**

***L*adies,**
Make God first in your life, and then watch your life reorganize itself with peace, even in the midst of life's storms.

March 11

My God, my God why hast thou forsaken me?
—**Matthew 27:46**

***L*adies,**
As Jesus hung on the cross, there was a time He felt all alone. But in that lonely time, Jesus did not get off the cross, because He knew His purpose and was obedient.

How many times have you experienced those lonely midnight hours when you felt no love, when you felt betrayed and abandoned? But in the midst of those moments, did you throw in the towel? No! Instead, He restored your soul. He led you in the paths of righteousness for His name's sake.

March 12

He made Him who knew no sin to be sin on our behalf that we might become the righteousness of God in Him.
—**2 Corinthians 5:21**

***L*adies,**
Jesus truly loves us, as he demonstrated on the cross. Thank God for His Son's unconditional love. There is no love like that on earth.

March 13

My God, My God why hast thou forsaken me.
—**<u>Matthew 27:46</u>**

***L*adies,**
Jesus died on the cross so we would never feel forsaken. When you put your trust and dependence on others, you expose your heart to abandonment or rejection. Put your trust in the Lord, and allow Him to hide your heart from Satan and his allies.

March 14

I Thirst
—**<u>John 19:28</u>**

***L*adies,**
Your personal relationship with God covers you from the thirst of your body. Thirst is a sinful craving for something that is not of God's will for you, which can lead you into damnation forever (hell).

Jesus' fifth word on the cross was proof that His suffering quenched our thirst.

March 15

In the last day, that great day of the feast, Jesus stood and cried, saying, if any man thirst, let him come unto me, and drink.
—**<u>John 7:37</u>**

***L*adies,**
Jesus provides all you need spiritually, physically, and emotionally. Trust and depend on Him and you shall never thirst again!

March 16

Whoever believes in me, as the scripture has said, streams of living water will flow from within him.
—**John 7:38**

***L*adies,**
Studying God's word will quench your thirst with happiness, because a close relationship with God brings complete peace and happiness like no other.

March 17 and 18

Father, into thy hands I commend my spirit.
—**Luke 23–46**

***L*adies,**
Jesus knew that once He died, His spirit would go on to God's kingdom. Jesus was saying, "Here I come, Father."

How certain are you that if you were to die tonight, you would go to heaven? If you are not certain, accept Christ into your life tonight. Remember it was not earthly man but God who kept you through all your uncertain times and circumstances in the previous year. You may be thinking right now that last year, at this time, your mind was cluttered, your heart was broken, and your spirit was defeated. But God kept you!

Praise God for His mercy!

March 19

It is finished
—**John 19:30**

***L*adies,**
Praise Jesus, praise Jesus, for His obedience, unconditional love, and faithfulness to sustain the agony and torment of the cross.

March 20 to 23

Father I entrust my spirit into your hands!
—**Luke 23:46**

***L*adies,**
When you complete a project, do you feel accomplished? Well, Jesus' sacrifice was the ultimate task, and He passed and because of His obedience he went back to glory with God.

In the next four days, beginning with today, read Jesus' last seven words:

1) "Father, forgive them, they don't know what they're doing (Luke 23:34),
2) I assure you, today you will be with me in paradise." (Luke 23:43),
3) Dear woman, here is your son." (John 19:26),
4) "My God, my God, why have you abandoned me?" (Mark 15: 34),
5) "I am thirsty" (John 19: 28),
6) "It is finished", (John 19:30),
7) Father I entrust my spirit into your hands!" (Luke 23: 46),

Study each Scripture, and apply it to your life as resurrection Sunday approaches.

Praise and honor to God almighty for His word!

March 24

And the multitudes that went before, and that followed, cried, saying Hosanna to the son of David: Blessed is he that cometh in the name of the Lord; Hosanna in the highest.
—**Matthew 21:9**

***L*adies,** our Savior is on the way. Give Him all praise and worship, for the time is near. Satan is anxious because God's people are touching the hearts of others and leading them to Christ.

March 25

Jesus said unto him, thou shalt love the Lord thy God with all thy heart, and with all thy soul, and with thy entire mind. This is the first and great commandment. And the second is like unto it, Thou shalt love thy neighbor as thyself.
—**Matthew 22:37–39**

***L*adies,**
Put God first and your heart will seek to do well to all.

March 26

Where there is no vision, the people perish: but he that keepeth the law, happy is he.
—**Proverbs 29:18**

***L*adies,**
Without God's guidance, we are subject to live in this world of chaos and disorder. But if we follow the law of God, our steps will lead us to God's everlasting peace. Follow the will of God for your life!

March 27

Watch and pray so that you will not fall into temptation, the spirit is willing, but the flesh is weak.
—**Mark 14:38**

***L*adies,**
Jesus asked the disciples to stay awake for only one hour while He prayed, but they fell asleep.

Do not allow your flesh to overrule your mind. Ask God to keep your mind regulated on Him and His Word; it shall not fail. In fact, it will protect you from Satan's scheming ways. Satan's temptation comes in all forms: depression ("Maybe this alcohol or drug will make me feel better"), suicide ("I have no purpose here anymore"), adultery ("My spouse does not love me anymore"), and stealing ("I need this money more than they do"). These are all lies that Satan can fill your head with daily if you do not stay alert. Pray. Pray for God's protection.

March 28

He went away a second time and prayed, "My father, if it is not possible for this cup to be taken away unless I drink it, may your will be done."
—**Matthew 26:42**

***L*adies,**
Jesus knew God could stop the crucifixion, but He trusted God and followed in God's will, not his own.
Continue to pray and ask God for guidance and strength during long-suffering days on your journey through life in God's will.

March 29

For God So Loved the World that He gave His one and only Son, that whoever believe in Him shall not perish but have eternal life.
—**John 3:16**

***L*adies,**
Our God loves us so much that He gave His precious son to suffer for us. Really? Think about it. Are you and I worthy? Are we serving God like we should or are we doing what makes us happy? Thank God that Jesus was obedient to His Father's will. Jesus saved us! We no longer have to worry about damnation to our souls, because Jesus the Savior saved us. Remember you are truly loved; there is no other love like God's love.

March 30

For you know that God paid a ransom to save you from the empty life you inherited from your ancestors. And the ransom he paid was not mere gold or silver. He paid for you with the precious lifeblood of Christ, the sinless, spotless Lamb of God.
—**1 Peter 1:18–19**

L**adies,**
Years ago, Jesus lay in a tomb—no fault of His but the fault of us. Jesus' faithfulness and love for us is incredible. Praise God!

March 31

Now after the Sabbath, as it came to dawn toward the first day of the week, Mary Magdalene and the other Mary came to look at the grave. And behold, a severe earthquake had occurred, for an angel of the Lord descended from heaven and came and rolled away the stone and sat upon it. And his appearance was like a lightening and his clothing as white as snow. The guards shook for fear of him and became like dead men. The angel said to the women, "Do not be afraid; for I know that you are looking for Jesus who has been crucified. He is not here, for He has just risen as He said. Come, see the place where He was lying. "Go quickly and tell His disciples that He has risen from the dead; and behold, He is going ahead of you into Galilee, there you will see Him; behold, I have told you." And they left the tomb and greeted them. And they came up and took hold of His feet and worshipped Him. Then Jesus said to them, "Do not be afraid; go and take word to my brethren to leave for Galilee, and there they will see Me."
—**Matthew 28:1–10**

L**adies,**
Jesus is risen! We no longer need to suffer, be disappointed, worry, or be fearful. The almighty God has raised our Savior, Jesus Christ. Jesus has paid the debt for our sins. We are saved! It is time to celebrate. Be joyful! Praise and honor to God; we made it through another month in this new year. Glory to God!

APRIL

Dose of Knowing

GOD IS KNOWING

April 1

This is the day which the Lord hath made; we will rejoice and be glad in it.
—**Psalm 118:24**

***L*adies,**
It is a new month in the new year! Jesus has saved us, and we can now go out and profess His love and saving power to all those who are lost. That is our mission for what He has done for us.

April 2

A new commandment I give unto you, That ye love one another; as I have loved you, that ye also love another.
—**John 13:34**

***L*adies,**
Be the role model in your families, and pour out love to all. On your daily journey, express and demonstrate love in all you do to all you meet. Let the light of Jesus shine.

April 3

With all lowliness and meekness, with longsuffering, forbearing one another in love;
—**Ephesians 4:2**

***L*adies,**
We humble ourselves, open our hearts and hands, and serve as Jesus served when He was here on Earth—that is our duty. Stop the selfishness; serve!

April 4

By this everyone will know that you are my disciples, if you love one another.
—**John 13:55**

***L*adies,**

The love Jesus was referring to was "agape love," which is sacrificial and unconditional regardless if love is reciprocated.

April 5

There are many devices in a man's heart; nevertheless the counsel of the Lord, that shall stand.

—**Proverbs 19:21**

***L*adies,**

God is in control. His purpose shall be revealed. Trust and wait on the Lord. Joy shall come in the morning—do not fret or faint.

April 6

Be still and know I am God.

—**Psalm 46:10**

And Moses said to the people, "Do not be afraid. Stand still, and see the salvation of the Lord, which He will accomplish for you today. For the Egyptians whom you see today, you shall see again no more forever.

—**Exodus 14:13**

***L*adies,**

Being still and trusting God will silence the Enemy, and he will know God is our rescuer. Being still is letting go of our controlling natures to allow all circumstances to be in God's hands, and it is trusting and waiting on God to work miracles. God is in control.

April 7

In all thy ways acknowledge him, and he shall direct thy paths.
—**Proverbs 3:6**

***L*adies,**
Give God all the honor and praise for everything in your lives (new day with new mercies, protection, job, home, food, good health, family, and friends). Without God, none of these things would be possible. Continue to allow God to direct your lives.

April 8

Train up a child in the way he should go; even when he is old, he will not depart from it.
—**Proverbs 22:6**

***L*adies,**
Our children are from God. No matter what our circumstances were when they came into this world (married, single, teen mother), God gave them to us. Children are gifts from God. I know some of you are thinking, "Really?" Yes, really. Even in those frantic moments of temper tantrums, hot tempers, and mouthy teens, they are gifts. Seek God's guidance while raising your children. Remember; do not conform to what or how the world says you should raise them. Seek God for direction.

April 9

In him we were also chosen, having been predestined according to the plan of him who works out everything in conformity with the purpose of his will.
—**Ephesians 1:11**

***L*adies,**
God is in Control. Your life was preplanned before the creation of the earth. Go to the throne of grace and ask God what His will (purpose) for your existence is. You will know your purpose when every step you take according to God's orders leads you to Him.

April 10

But he said to me, "My grace is sufficient for you, for my power is made perfect in weakness."
—**2 Corinthians 12:9**

***L*adies,**
When you are weak, just call on the Lord. He will provide you with the strength you need to make it through. Your calling can be one word: Jesus. There's power in that name!

April 11

Therefore God also has highly exalted him and given him the name which is above Every name, that at the name of Jesus every knee shall bow, of those in heaven and of those on earth, and of those under the earth, and that every tongue should confess that Jesus Christ is Lord, to the glory of God the Father.
—**Philippians 2:9–11**

***L*adies,**
The only name that you should call on is Jesus.

April 12

Whoever walks with the wise becomes wise, but the companion of fools will suffer harm.
—**Proverbs 13:20**

***L*adies,**
Ask Jesus to lead you in all you do. Be cautious of those who are lost, no matter who they are: family, friends, or coworkers.

April 13

And my God will supply every need of yours according to his riches in glory in Christ Jesus.
—**Philippians 4:19**

***L*adies,**
Our God is a provider. Trust Him and it shall be done!

April 14

Let everything that hath breath Praise The Lord!
Praise ye The Lord.
—**Psalm 150:6**

***L*adies,**
Praise Him!

April 15

That your Faith should not stand in the wisdom of men But in the power of God!
—**1 Corinthians 2:5**

***L*adies,**
True faith is sincerely trusting God and waiting for God to manifest His miracle to your human eyes.

April 16

"Because he loves me," says the Lord, "I will rescue him; I will protect him, for he acknowledge my name."
—**<u>Psalm 91:14</u>**

***L*adies,**
God can and will protect you from the evilness that plagues our world. Trust Him and depend on Him.

April 17

For we walk by faith, not by sight
—**<u>2 Corinthians 5:7</u>**

***L*adies,**
Do not allow time to diminish your hope, no matter how long it takes. God has given you a promise, and He will sustain you until you are to receive that promise. Stay faithful to God!

April 18 and 19

These trials are Only to test your Faith, to show that It is strong and pure. It is being tested as fire tests and purifies gold ... and your faith is far more precious to God than mere gold. So if your faith Remains strong after being tried by fiery trials, it will bring you much praise and glory and honor on the day when Jesus Christ is revealed to the whole world.
—**<u>1 Peter 1:7</u>**

***L*adies,**
It is only a test.

April 20

Be Alert and sober minded. Your enemy the devil prowls around like a roaring lion looking for someone to devour. Resist him, standing firm in the faith, because you know that the family of believers throughout the world is undergoing the same kind of sufferings. And the God of all grace, who called you to his eternal glory in Christ, after you have suffered a little while, will himself Restore you and make you Strong, Firm and Steadfast. To Him be the power forever and forever. Amen.
—**1 Peter 5:8–10**

***L*adies,**
This world may be full of Satan's allies, but God's power reigns! Pray for God's sustaining power.

April 21 and 22

Whoever says he abides in him ought to walk in the same way in which he walked.
—**1 John 2:6**

To put off your old self, which is belongs to your former manner of life and is corrupt through deceitful desires, and to be renewed in the spirit of your minds, and to put on the new self, created after the likeness of God in true righteousness and holiness.
—**Ephesians 4:22–24**

***L*adies,**
What would Jesus do?

We need to continually ask ourselves that question in all circumstances *before* we act. Is it an easy question? No, but is it possible? Yes, with God all things are possible. Being a Christian is a daily walk. Remember, you are not walking alone. God's presence is in front of and beside you, carrying you along the way.

April 23

Awake, thou that sleepest, and arise from the dead, and Christ shall give thee light.
—**Ephesians 5:14**

***L*adies,**
Allow your soul to break free and illuminate. The Light of Christ shall guide your every footstep.

April 24

Jesus answered him, "Truly, truly, I say to you, unless one is born again he cannot see the kingdom of God."
—**John 3:3**

***L*adies,**
Rebirth—belief in Jesus as our Savior is a guarantee of an everlasting, peaceful life. Nothing on this earth will remain with us, not illness, depression from job loss, death of loved ones, divorce, rejection, or betrayal. Life adversities will remain here on earth, not in heaven.

April 25

Rejoice in hope, be patient in tribulation, be constant in prayer.
—**Romans 12:12**

***L*adies,**
This excerpt comes out of Elizabeth Lesser's book, *Broken Open*:

> When we descend all the way down to the bottom of a loss, and dwell patiently with an open heart, in the darkness and pain, we can bring back up with us the sweetness of life and exhilaration of inner growth. When there is nothing left to lose, we the true self … the self that is whole, the self that is enough, the self that no longer looks to

others for definition, or completion, or anything but companionship on the journey.

Amen!

April 26

The Lord shall fight for you and ye shall hold your peace.
—**Exodus 14:14**

***L*adies,**
Be still in the midst of your circumstances. Being still allows you to listen to God for direction. Chaos causes more conflict. Be still; take a moment and spend it with God, releasing your burdens to the One who can carry them away.

April 27

For God alone, O my soul, wait in silence, for my hope is from him.
—**Psalm 62:5**

***L*adies,**
Be still and listen to the Almighty speak.

April 28

But Without Faith it is impossible to please him; for he that cometh to God must believe that He is a rewarder of them that diligently seek him.
—**Hebrews 11:6**

***L*adies,**
Your faith pleases God over anything else. So, put your trust in God, sit back, and watch Him move in your life.

April 29

And we know that for those who love God all things work together for good, for those who are called according to His purpose.
—**Romans 8:28**

***L*adies,**
God is in control.

April 30

Many are the plans in a person's heart, but it is the Lord's purpose that Prevails.
—**Proverbs 19:21**

***L*adies,**
God's will, God's way—He is in control.

MAY

Dose of

TRUSTING GOD

May 1

Therefore, since we have been made right in God's sight by faith, we have peace with God because of what Jesus Christ our Lord has done for us.
—**Romans 5:1**

***L*adies,**
Faith brings peace. Continue to have faith in the almighty God and His peace shall cover you!

May 2

Without faith it is impossible to please God.
—**Hebrews 11:6**

***L*adies,**
Our relationship with the Lord is dependent on our faith in God.

May 3

Guard my life, for I am devoted to you. You are my God; save your servant who trusts in you.
—**Psalm 86:2**

***L*adies,**
Do you trust God to save you?

May 4

Whoever is kind to the poor lends to the Lord, and He will reward them for what they have done.
—**Proverbs 19:17**

Ladies,
God offers grace and mercy when we extend love to others, and God's radiating light is shown through us.

May 5

Who hath delivered us from the power of darkness, and hath translated us into the kingdom of his dear Son; in whom we have redemption through his blood, even the forgiveness of sins:
—**Colossians 1:13–14**

Ladies,
You are broken open and can now blossom into who you were predestined to be. Jesus brought you out of darkness!

May 6

Every word of God is pure: He is a shield unto them that put their trust in Him.
—**Proverbs 30:5**

Ladies,
Trust Jesus. His death on the cross covered us.

May 7

And he said to the woman, Thy Faith hath saved thee; Go in peace.
—**Luke 7:50**

Ladies,
When it appears that all hope is gone, call out the name of Jesus, and watch His miraculous works begin.

May 8

That your faith should not stand in the wisdom of men, but in the Power of God!
—**1 Corinthians 2:5**

L**adies,**
Stop thinking the world (family, friends, job, or even you) is going to resolve your problems. Only God can handle them. Put your faith in Him—trust Him.

May 9

And after you have suffered a little while, the God of all grace, who had called you to his eternal glory in Christ, will himself restore, confirm, strengthen and establish you.
—**1 Peter 5:10**

L**adies,**
After the storm comes the sunlight.

May 10

To Him be the power for ever and ever Amen.
—**1 Peter 5:11**

L**adies,**
God has everlasting power.

May 11

For God hath not given us the spirit of fear, but of Power and of Love and of a Sound mind.
—**2 Timothy 1:7**

***L*adies,**
No matter what challenges you face today, there is no fear with God on your side.

May 12

Charm is deceptive, and beauty is fleeting; but a woman who fears the Lord is to be praised!
—**<u>Proverbs 31:30</u>**

A kindhearted woman gains respect.
—**<u>Proverbs 11:6</u>**

Happy Mother's Day!

May 13

I will restore to you the years that the locust has eaten.
—**<u>Joel 2:25</u>**

***L*adies,**
Do not fret about wasted time—days, months, or even years—broken by the Enemy. God can restore all that He intended for you. Trust Him, and wait on the Lord.

May 14

Therefore if any man be in Christ, he is a new creature; old things are passed away; behold all things are become new. And all things are of God, who hath reconciled us to himself by Jesus Christ, and hath given to us the ministry of reconciliation; To wit, that God was in Christ, reconciling the world unto himself, not imputing their trespasses unto them; and hath committed unto us the word of reconciliation. Now that we are ambassadors for Christ, as though God did beseech you by us; we pray you in Christ's stead, by ye reconciled to God.
—**<u>2 Corinthians 5:17</u>**

***L*adies,**
Reconcile with God. He sent Jesus to Earth to save us from eternal hell. When you show God how He is first in your life, God's will shall manifest.

May 15

Peace I leave with you; my peace I now give to you. Not as the world gives do I give to you. Do not let your hearts be troubled, neither let them be afraid.
—John 14:27

***L*adies,**
Stop allowing yourselves to be agitated and disturbed, and do not permit yourselves to be fearful, intimidated, cowardly, and unsettled. Trust God.

May 16

And the fruit of righteousness is sown in peace of them that make peace.
—James 3:18

***L*adies,**
Display your peace to all today.

May 17

The Lord is my Rock and my Fortress and my Deliverer; my God, my strength in whom I will trust!!
—Psalm 18:2

***L*adies,**
Trust Him!

May 18

Now Faith is the substance of things hoped for, the evidence of things not seen.
—**Hebrews 11:1**

***L*adies,**
Continue walking with Christ. Do not fret about where He's taking you; just have faith, and watch the miracles of God come forth!

May 19

Your eyes saw my unformed body; all the days ordained for me were written in your book before one of them came to be.
—**Psalm 139:16**

***L*adies,**
God predestined your life. Trust His will for your life.

May 20

Therefore, my dear brothers and sisters Stand firm. Let Nothing move you, always give yourselves fully to the work of the Lord. Because you know the work of the Lord is not in vain.
—**1 Corinthians 15:58**

***L*adies,**
Despite the wicked ways of others, continue to move forward toward God's promises for your life.

May 21

He gives strength to the weary and increases the power of the weak.
—**Isaiah 40:29**

***L*adies,**
Hold onto God's unchanging hand; the Devil will use his allies to try to pull you away.

May 22

And the world passeth away, and the lust thereof; But she that doth the will of God abideth forever.
—1 John 2:17

***L*adies,**
Focus on the works of the almighty God.

May 23

Be Sober, Be Vigilant; because your adversary the devil, as a roaring lion, walketh about, seeking whom he can devour.
—1 Peter 5:8

***L*adies,**
Stay alert at all times, those people or moments that you want to bring you joy are only temporary. Remove the facade. Everlasting joy is with Jesus. Do not allow Satan to invade your minds with envy, bitterness, or an unforgiving heart, which will devour.
Instead, trust, depend, and seek the ways of Christ.

May 24

Don't worry about anything; instead, pray about everything. Tell God what you need, and thank him for all he has done. Then you will experience God's peace, which exceeds anything we can understand. His peace will guard your hearts and minds as you live in Christ.
—Philippians 4:6–7

***L*adies,**
Stop worrying! You serve a mighty God who can handle anything and everything.

May 25

And Jesus looking upon them saith, With men it is impossible, But with God: for with God All things are possible!
—**Mark 10:27**

***L*adies,**
Stop depending on the world. Only God can resolve any circumstance you are dealing with. Trust God!

May 26

These things I have spoken unto you, that in me ye might have peace. In the world ye shall have tribulation: but be of good cheer; I have overcome the world.
—**John 16:33**

***L*adies,**
In God's presence and with God's perfect peace, you can face uncertainty.

May 27

Every way of a man is right in his own eyes: but the Lord pondereth the hearts.
—**Proverbs 21:2**

***L*adies,**
You may fool yourself and others, but God knows your heart.

May 28

I say then: Walk in the Spirit, and you shall not fulfill the lust of the flesh. If we live in the Spirit, let us also walk in the Spirit.
—**Galatians 5:16**

***L*adies,**
How many times have you wanted to give a piece of your mind to someone who made you mad? How many times have you wanted to stop waiting on God to answer your prayer and resolve the issue yourself? How many times have you wanted to live in the moment and forget about being a responsible adult?
Remember, when those flesh moments are staring you in the face, call on the name of Jesus, and He shall rescue you, without a doubt!
Trust Him.

May 29

And Jesus answered them, "Truly, I say to you, if you have faith and do not doubt, you will not only do what has been done to the fig tree, but even if you say to the mountain, be taken up and thrown into the sea," it will happen.
—**Matthew 21:21**

***L*adies,**
Do not allow this world and Satan's negative, none-trusting allies to put doubt in your mind. Instead, have faith, and keep your eyes on God. Stay in His presence and enjoy the peace.

May 30

Thou hast turned for me my mourning into dancing, thou hast put off my sackcloth, and girded me with gladness.
—**Psalm 30:11**

***L*adies,**
Praise God for a new day of infinite blessings.

May 31

But Jesus turned him about, and when he saw her, he said, Daughter, be of good comforth; thy faith hath made thee whole. And the woman was made whole from that hour.
—**Matthew 9:22**

***L*adies,**
Have you trusted God this month? Did you relentlessly seek Him? God wants your dependence to be on Him only. God can provide you with your blessings.

JUNE

Dose of

WALKING WITH GOD

June 1

For I the Lord thy God will Hold thy right hand, saying unto thee, fear not; I will help thee.
—**Isaiah 41:13**

***L*adies,**
In this new month, hold God's unchanging hand. Welcome His presence every day as you journey on. As you walk with Him, watch and feel His presence embrace you. Praise the Lord.

June 2

And this is the confidence that we have toward him, that if we ask anything according to his will he hears us. And if we know that he hears us in whatever we as, we know that we have the requests that we have asked him.
—**1 John 5:14–15**

***L*adies,**
God answers prayers!

June 3

Trust in the Lord with all thine heart; and lean not unto thine own understanding.
—**Proverbs 3:5**

***L*adies,**
Keep your eyes on God and not the world so that you are not redirected.
Stay focused on God and He shall direct your path.

June 4

I can do all things through Christ which strengthen me.
—**Philippians 4:13**

***L*adies,**
Grip God's unchanging hand tight, and stay in close communication with Him. The Enemy wants to devour. God will keep you in perfect peace when challenging times are present.

June 5

Set your affection on things above, not on things on the earth.
—**Colossians 3:2**

***L*adies,**
Put on blinders to distract yourselves from the concerns of the world and continue your walk with God. This will strengthen your trust and dependence on Him.

June 6

Blessed is the woman who remains steadfast under trial, for when she has stood the test she will Receive the crown of life, which God has promised to those who love him.
—**James 1:12**

***L*adies,**
Stand and wait on God; He shall not fail.

June 7

Lord, you are my God; I will exalt you and praise your name, for in perfect faithfulness you have done marvelous things, things planned long ago.
—**Isaiah 25:1**

***L*adies,**
Praise God; He is faithful!

June 8

And we know that for those who love God all things work together for good, for those who are called according to his purpose.
—**Romans 8:28**

***L*adies,**
Trust that God is sovereignly working out each trial in your life for your best.

June 9

Don't worry about anything; instead pray about everything. Tell God what you need and thank him for all he has done. Then you will experience God's peace, which exceeds anything we can understand. His peace will guard your hearts and minds as you live in Christ Jesus.
—**Philippians 4:6–7**

***L*adies,**
It is simple:

Pray + ask + thank God = God's peace.

June 10 and 11

And let the peace of God rule in your hearts, to the which also ye are called in one body; and be ye thankful.
—**Colossians 3:15**

***L*adies,**
Ask God to come into your hearts and minds so you may experience God's goodness. Repeat this verse two days in a row. Why? Because thanking God brings forth peace!

June 12

For she walk by faith, not by sight.
—**2 Corinthians 5:7**

***L*adies,**
Keep your eyes focused on God!

June 13

But without faith it is impossible to please him; for she cometh to God must believe that He is a rewarder of them that diligently seek him.
—**Hebrews 11:6**

***L*adies,**
Close your ears to naysayers and those who doubt God's ability. Continue to trust that God will make a way in all circumstances.

June 14

But he turned and said to Peter, "Get behind me, Satan! You are a hinderance to me; you do not have in mind the concerns of God, but merely human concerns.
—**Matthew 16:23**

***L*adies,**
Do not listen to naysayers (family or friends) whose conversations lack faith. Satan is using them to break the bond you have established with God on trusting Him with all.

June 15

But remember the Lord your God. He gives you the ability to produce wealth. That shows he stands by the terms of his covenant. He promised it with an oath to your people long ago. And he's still faithful to his covenant today.
—**Deuteronomy 8:18**

***L*adies,**
God will show you a way to meet all your needs. The way is God.

June 16

Though I walk in the midst of trouble, you preserve my life; you stretch out your hand against the wrath of my enemies, and your right hand delivers me.
—**Psalm 138:7**

Train up a child in the way he should go; and when he is old he will not depart from it.
—**Proverbs 22:6**

***L*adies,**
Satan wants our children, but God will cover them from Satan's scheming plans. Pray for God's protection over them daily.

June 17

So do not worry, saying, "What shall we eat? or what shall we drink? or what shall we wear? for the pagans run after these things and your heavenly Father knows that you need them.
—**Matthew 6:31–32**

***L*adies,** stop fretting. God never fails. In the nick of time, He provides! Amen.

June 18

Look at the birds of the air. They don't plant or gather crops. They don't put away crops in storerooms. But your Father who is in heaven feeds them. Aren't you worth much more than they are?
—**Matthew 6:26**

***L*adies,**
God loves you and will provide.

June 19

And give no opportunity to the devil.
—**Ephesians 4:27**

For God is not a God of confusion but of peace. As in the churches of the saints.
—**1 Corinthians 14:33**

***L*adies,**
Do not allow non-Christians to speak against the teachings of our Savior. Stay in the Word of God!

June 20

And after you have suffered a little while, the God of all grace, who has called you to his eternal glory in Christ, will himself restore, confirm, strengthen and establish you.
—**1 Peter 5:10**

***L*adies,**
Once God allows you to leap over that hurdle (life circumstance), you will feel a sense of restoration and peace.

June 21

Sing to God. Sing Praise to His holy name. Lift up a song to the one who rides on the clouds. His name is Lord. Be glad when you are with Him.
—**Psalm 68:4**

***L*adies,**
Sing and praise about God's goodness in your lives. Shout to all how merciful He is.

June 22 and 23

For I the Lord thy God will hold thy right hand, saying unto thee, Fear not; I will help thee.
—**Isaiah 41:13**

***L*adies,**
In the midst of life circumstances, keep your eyes on God.
This Scripture was repeated because the Enemy is failing. He is desperately looking for new ways to detour God's daughters. Stay focused!

June 24

Know therefore that the Lord thy God, He is God, the faithful God, which keepeth covenant and mercy with them that love him and keep his commandments to a thousand generations.
—**Deuteronomy 7:9**

***L*adies,**
When unforeseen blessings happen in your lives, praise God for loving you and providing for you.

June 25

My soul, wait thou only upon God; for my expectation is from Him. He only is my rock and my salvation; He is my defense; I shall not be moved.
—**Psalm 62:5–6**

***L*adies,**
Whatever it is you need from God, wait on Him to supply it. But remember, all blessings from God are given so that you can honor God, not yourself or earthly man (job, spouse, friend, or family). God gets the praise!
Remember, if what you want or need does not bring praise to God, it will not come forth into a blessing.

June 26

The Lord is my shepherd; I shall not want. He maketh me to lie down in green pastures; he leadeth me beside the still waters. He restoreth my soul; he leadeth me in the paths of righteousness for his name's sake. Yea, though I walk through the valley of the shadow of death. I will fear no evil for thou art with me, thy rod and thy staff they comfort me.
—**Psalm 23:1–4**

***L*adies,**
When our minds are consumed with God, we can endure anything!

June 27 and 28

No weapon formed against you shall prosper, and every tongue which rises against you in judgment You shall condemn. This is the heritage of the servants of the Lord, and their righteousness is from me says the Lord.
—**Isaiah 54:17**

We must focus our eyes on Jesus, the author and finisher of our faith.
—**Hebrews 12:2**

***L*adies,**

The Devil and his allies are upset that despite worldly trials, we remain faithful and focused on God, and His peace comforts us. Continue to follow God's plan.

June 29 and 30

Though the mountains be shaken and the hills be removed, yet my unfailing love for you will not be shaken nor my covenant of peace be removed, says the Lord who has compassion on you.

—**Isaiah 54:10**

***L*adies,**

Peace is upon you if you walk with God.

JULY

Dose of

PEACE IN THE PRESENCE OF GOD

July 1

Make me to know your ways, O Lord; teach me your paths. Lead me in your truth and teach me, for you are the God of my salvation; for you I wait all the day long.
—**Psalm 25:4–5**

***L*adies,**
Sit in the presence of God, and wait for Him to direct your next step. Stay focused!

July 2

You will show me the path of life; in thy presence is fullness of joy; at thy right hand there are pleasures for evermore.
—**Psalm 16:11**

***L*adies,**
Stay in the presence of the Lord and experience a joyful heart.

July 3

The Lord be with all of you.
—**2 Thessalonians 3:16**

***L*adies,**
Allow God's presence to be with you now and forever.

July 4

Stand fast therefore in the liberty wherewith Christ hath made us Free, and be Not entangled again with the yoke of bondage.
—**Galatians 5:1**

Ladies,
Liberate yourself from all worries, and rest in the presence of the almighty God. He removes the shackles of life; dance and praise Him!

July 5

And the peace of God, which passeth all understanding, shall keep your hearts and minds through Christ Jesus.
—**Philippians 4:7**

Ladies,
Peace is a state of tranquility or quiet, freedom from civil disturbance, according to *Merriam Webster*. But it is ultimately a gift from God. The presence of peace in your lives indicates God's blessings on you from your obedience and faith.

July 6 and 7

I will instruct thee and teach thee in the way which thou shalt go: I will guide thee with mine eye.
—**Psalm 32:8**

Ladies,
As the days proceed on, many circumstances will attempt to lead you astray from the direction that God has for you. Stay focused on God and His way. The Enemy is busy trying to defeat the plans God has in store for you.

July 8

Be still, and know that I am God!
—**Psalm 46:10**

Ladies,
Leave your sorrows and burdens with God, and just be still.

July 9

Blessed are they that mourn; for they shall be comforted.
—**Matthew 5:4**

***L*adies,**
Each day is precious and tomorrow is not promised, so express your love today!

July 10

Surely goodness and mercy shall follow me all the days of my life and I will dwell in the house of the Lord forever.
—**Psalm 23:6**

***L*adies,**
Know that God has you covered.

July 11

For by Grace you have been saved through Faith. And this is not your own doing; it is the Gift of God!
—**Ephesians 2:8**

***L*adies,**
Your faith shall free you from bondage by the grace of God, which is a gift from God for your obedience in following His will. So, do not fret, but trust in the almighty God to bring you through.

July 12

The righteous cry, and the Lord heareth, and delivereth them out of all their troubles. The Lord is nigh unto them that are of a broken heart; and saveth such as be of contrite spirit. Many are the afflictions of the righteous; but the Lord

delivereth him out of them all. He keepeth all his bones; not one of them is broken. Evil shall slay the wicked and they that hate the righteous shall be desolate. The Lord Redeemeth the soul of his servants; and none of them that trust in him shall be desolate.
—**Psalm 34:17–22**

***L*adies,**
God will save you from all your troubles and protect you from Satan's allies in this world. Serve the Lord!

July 13

Behold, children are a heritage from the Lord, the fruit of the womb is his reward.
—**Psalm 127:3**

***L*adies,**
Our children are gifts from God, and we should train them up to love and serve God all the days of their lives.

July 14

Thou wilt shew me the path of life: in thy presence is fullness of joy; at thy right hand there are pleasures for evermore.
—**Psalm 16:11**

The steps of a good woman are ordered by the Lord: and He delighteth in her way. Though she fall, she shall not be utterly cast down; for the Lord upholdeth her with his hand.
—**Psalm 37:23–24**

***L*adies,**
Hold tight to God's unchanging right hand, and allow Him to lead you. The road may be bumpy and the mountains high, but God has a mighty blessing waiting for you if you trust and depend on Him.

July 15 and 16

So don't worry. Don't say, What will we eat? Or what will we drink? or what will we wear? People who are ungodly run after all of those things. Your Father who is in heaven knows that you need them. But put God's kingdom first. Do what he wants you to do. Then all of those things will also be given to you. So don't worry about tomorrow. Tomorrow will worry about itself. Each day has enough trouble of its own.
—**Matthew 6:31–34**

***L*adies,**
Has God not provided for you in the past? So, why do you fret over the next financial challenge that is presently in your life? God has already paid it in full. Trust and know God will provide all you need. Live each day focused on God, and all around you will become a mere thought. Why? Because God is handling everything for you, which means you do not have to worry; He's taking care of things.

July 17

For to be carnally minded is death; but to be spiritually minded is life and peace.
—**Romans 8:6**

***L*adies,**
Strive to be spiritually minded. Ask the Holy Spirit to guide you. A carnally minded person is self-interested, self-indulgent, and self-sufficient. There is no peace in a selfish lifestyle. Spiritually minded people put God in the center of their lives and seek His will. God is their sufficiency. When you release all to Him, peace will embrace your mind and body.

July 18

And others save with fear, pulling them out of the fire; hating even the garment spotted by the flesh. Now unto him that is able to keep you from falling, and to present you faultless before the presence of his glory with exceeding joy. To the

only wise God our Saviour, be glory and majesty, dominion and power, both now and ever. Amen.
—**Jude 1:23–25**

***L*adies,**
Show mercy to those in doubt, and pull sinners out of Satan's hands by professing God's goodness and faithfulness. Always give God praise.

July 19

For satan himself masquerades as an angel of light.
—**2 Corinthians 11:14**

***L*adies,**
Not all that shines is from God. Beware!

July 20

Seek the Lord and His strength: seek his face continually.
—**Psalm 105:4**

***L*adies,**
Seeking the Lord will bring you all you need. Try Jesus!

July 21

For God is not a God of disorder but of peace. As in all the congregations of the saints.
—**1 Corinthians 14:33**

***L*adies,**
When the power of love overcomes the love of power, the world will know peace that only God can deliver (paraphrased from Jimi Hendrix).

July 22

Love not the world, neither the things that are in the world. If any man love the world, the love of the Father is not in him. For all that is in the world, the lust of the flesh, and the lust of the eyes, and the pride of life, is not of the Father, but is of the world. And the world passeth away, and the lust thereof; but he that doeth the will of God abideth forever.
—**1 John 2:15–17**

***L*adies,**
Do not focus on people or things that are not of God.

Not of God: People who want to control your actions and thoughts. People who are self-serving, people who are unforgiving, and people who do not believe that Jesus died for us and is our Savior.

July 23

I will praise the Lord all my life. I will sing to my God as long as I live. Don't put your trust in human leaders. Don't trust in people. They can't save you. When they die, they return to the ground. On that very day their plans are bound to fail. Blessed are those who depend on the God of Jacob for help. Blessed are those who put their hope in the Lord their God.
—**Psalm 146:2–5**

***L*adies,**
Earthly beings will fail you; stop looking for a savior in man. Jesus is the only Savior.

July 24

Blessed is the man that heareth me, watching daily at my gates, waiting at the posts of my doors. For whoso findeth me findeth life, and shall obtain favour of the Lord.
—**Proverbs 8:34–35**

***L*adies,**
When you find Jesus, you find joy and insurmountable peace!

July 25

Casting all your anxieties on him, because he cares for you.
—1 Peter 5:7

***L*adies,**
Stop. Stop focusing on your trials. Trust God.

July 26 and 27

But mine eyes are unto thee, O God the Lord in thee is my trust, leave not my soul destitute.
—Psalm 14:8

***L*adies,**
Look to the Lord, and trust that He will never leave you, ever.

July 28

Come to Me, all who are weary and heavy-laden, and I will give you rest. Take my yoke upon you and learn from Me, for I am gentle and humble in heart; and you shall find rest for your souls. For My yoke is easy, and my load is light.
—Matthew 11:28–30

***L*adies,**
Rest and be still in the Lord, and allow Him to give you sustaining peace.

July 29

Now may the Lord of Peace himself continually grant you peace in every circumstance. The Lord be with you all.

***L*adies,**
To know Jesus is to know peace.

July 30

And the Lord will deliver me from every evil work and preserve me for His heavenly kingdom. To him be glory forever and ever. Amen.
—**2 Timothy 4:18**

***L*adies,**
Do not let evil people steal any more blessings meant for you. Pray for them without judgment. No weapon formed against thee shall prosper.

July 31

For God does not show favoritism.
—**Romans 2:11**

***L*adies,**
If you want joy and peace in your life, stop envying others. God loves us all equally.

AUGUST

Dose of

AWAKENING

August 1 and 2

Nor height, nor depth, nor any other creature, shall be able to separate us from the Love of God which is in Christ Jesus our Lord.
—**Romans 8:38–39**

***L*adies,**
Nothing can separate you from God. Misery often stems from the feeling of being unloved. Well, listen up! Even if you have experienced or are experiencing an earthly love, there is no greater unconditional love like Christ's love. He will never forsake you.

August 3 and 4

You make known to me the path of life; in your presence there is fullness of joy; at your right hand are pleasures forevermore.
—**Psalm 16:11**

***L*adies,**
Joy is Jesus!

August 5

I will make you stronger. You will be like a garden that has plenty of water.
—**Isaiah 58:11**

***L*adies,**
Jesus is strength!

August 6 and 7

Dear friends, you are outsiders and strangers in this world. So I am asking you not to give in to your sinful longings. They fight against your soul. People who don't believe might say you are doing wrong. But lead good lives among them. Then they will see your good works. And they will give glory to God on the day he comes to judge.
—1 Peter 2:11

L**adies,**
Sit quietly in the presence of God, and do not fret about today or even tomorrow. Sit in God's sufficiency as the chaos moves around you.

August 8

Preach the word. Be ready to do it whether it is convenient or inconvenient. Correct, confront and encourage with patience and instruction.
—2 Timothy 4:2

L**adies,**
In order to minister to others, you must first stay in the word. Only provide God's word, not your opinion. We are just vessels. God speaks through us.

August 9

Trust in the Lord with all your heart. Do not depend on your own understanding.
—Proverbs 3:5

L**adies,**
Understanding will never bring you peace. Stop trying to master your life. This life is filled with endless problems. Seek God, the master of all problems. God's love is not elusive. You are always enveloped in His peace, which you can find in His presence.

August 10

See then that you walk circumspectly, not as fools but as wise, redeeming the time, because the days are evil.
—**Ephesians 5:15–16**

***L*adies,**
Focus on what is truly important: God.
As you center your thoughts more on Him, all your fears and worries will go away because God provides peace of mind that surpasses all. God can and will handle all; trust Him.

August 11

For what shall it profit a woman, if she shall gain the whole world and lose her own soul?
—**Mark 8:36**

***L*adies,**
Is your soul for sale?
Sale: Promiscuity, jealousy, backbiting, bitterness, unforgiveness, negativity, and dependence on earthly things or people, as well as being unloving, being selfish, or abandoning children (physically, emotionally).

God is forgiving and loves you. Become the woman of God that He destined you to be: virtuous, trusting, encouraging, supportive, joyful, forgiving, positive, loving, generous, and dependent only on God.

August 12 and 13

After Herod arrested Peter, he put him in prison, Peter was placed under guard. He was watched by four groups of four soldiers each. Herod planned to put Peter on public trial. It would take place after the Passover Feast.

So Peter was kept in Prison. But the church prayed hard to God for him. It was the night before Herod was going to bring him to trial. Peter was sleeping between soldiers. Two chains held him there. Suddenly an Angel of The Lord appeared. A light shone in the prison cell. The angel struck Peter on his side. Peter woke up. Quick, the angel said, Get up, the chains fell off Peter's wrist. Then the angel said to him, put on your clothes and sandals. Peter did so. Peter followed him out of the prison. But he had no idea that what the angel was doing was really happening. He thought he was seeing a vision. They passed the first and second guards. Then they came to the iron gate leading to the city. It opened for them by itself. They went through it.
—**Acts 12:4–10**

***L*adies,**
Is God trying to move you into a new season in your life? God has opened the door to your destiny. Take hold of His hand and walk into it. Do not fear or doubt; trust God!

August 14

And I will give you a new heart, and a new spirit I will put within you. And I will remove the heart of stone from your flesh and give you a heart of flesh.
—**Ezekiel 36:26**

***L*adies,**
Release the old ways—stubbornness and unforgiveness. Instead, open your hearts to the unconditional love of God so you can respond with love and patience with all you encounter.

August 15

Every good gift and every perfect gift is from above, coming down from the Father of lights with whom there is no variation or shadow due to change.
—**James 1:17**

Ladies,
Praise God for all the blessings He has showered you with and those that are coming in your new season.

August 16 and 17

The heart of a woman plans her way, but the Lord establishes her steps.
—**Proverbs 16:9**

Ladies,
Whatever you dream of for your future, allow God to direct your steps. If it's His plan, it shall be done.

August 18

Iron sharpens iron, and one woman sharpens another.
—**Proverbs 27:17**

Ladies,
Ask God to bless you with friends who are spiritually like-minded, loyal, and servants of God.

August 19

For all have sinned and fall short of the glory of God.
—**Romans 3:23**

Ladies,
There is not one sinless person walking this earth. Do not be fooled by the phony people who portray their lives as perfect. Jesus was the only perfect person who walked this earth. Do not envy or covet another woman's anything—not her life, job, spouse, children, house, car, or anything else. Nothing is perfect!

The Enemy, Satan, wants to trick you into distrusting God when you think your life is not mimicking another woman's life. Be careful. Walk into the destiny God has for you and your blessings will come.

August 20

I know thy works; behold, I have set before thee an open door, and no man can shut it; for thou hast a little strength, and hast kept my word, and hast not denied my word.
—**Revelation 3:8**

Ladies,
The door is open. Fear is a trick of the Enemy. Walk through and experience God's love and blessings.

August 21

I have told the glad news of deliverance in the great congregation; behold I have not restrained my lips, as you know, O Lord. I have not hidden your deliverance within my heart, I have spoken of your faithfulness and your salvation; I have not concealed your steadfast love and your faithfulness from the great congregation.
—**Psalm 40:9–10**

Ladies,
Are you ashamed to testify about God's saving grace in your lives? Are you ashamed to tell others how you were delivered from promiscuity? How God saved you from drugs, forgave you after aborting a child, or kept your mind when you had a miscarriage and no biological children? Are you ashamed to tell others how God forgave you when you divorced your husband? How He saved your marriage and healed your body after a double mastectomy?

We are here to praise God to the world, not in secret. Women are dying and going to hell because we are concerned about how our family and friends perceive us. Serve God and testify.

August 22

Let your eyes look straight ahead. Keep looking right in front of you.
—**Proverbs 4:25**

L**adies,**
Focus on God and peace shall follow.

August 23

Bear ye one another's burdens, and so fulfill the law of Christ.
—**Galatians 6:2**

L**adies,**
Do you have what is called the burden-bearer personality? God created you in His own image and gave you a loving heart. He designed your heart to feel what He feels and to feel what others feel. God created you to empathize with Him and His children. He meant for you to lift up your burdens to Him and trust that He will take care of everything. He meant life to be light for you because of your unshakable trust in Him. You should be generous. Your generosity can change people's lives. God admires your heart so much that He delights in giving you the opportunity to partner with Him in sharing His love to those in need. God gifted you with the ability to restore joy to His hurting children.

What is the burden that God has placed on you?
Counseling battered women?
Counseling women in prison?
Counseling teen mothers?
Counseling women on drugs/alcohol?
Counseling women in bad marriages?
Counseling women with health issues?

Whatever it is, just do it, and do it with the Word of God.

August 24

Who can find a virtuous woman? She is far more precious than jewels. Strength and honor are her clothing. and she can laugh at the time to come. She opens her mouth with wisdom, and loving instruction is on her tongue. She watches over the activities of her household and is never idle. Her sons rise up and call her blessed. Her husband also praises her: Many women are capable, but you surpass them all. Charm is deceptive and beauty is fleeting, but a woman who fears the Lord will be praised.
—**Proverbs 31:10, 25–30**

Ladies,
Do you know a woman who is like what Proverbs 31 describes? Is it your mom, grandmother, aunt, sister, or friend? Is it you?

August 25

There is One lawgiver, who is able to save and to destroy; who art thou that judge another?
—**James 4:12**

Ladies,
Judgment is for God!
Stop commenting on something or someone who does not fit your mind-set of how things or people should act! You do not control anyone, including your children. If the people of this world would focus on God, there would be less chaos.

Chaos: children seeking love outside of their homes and becoming part of a gang, seeking acceptance, marriages ending in divorce because power is being demonstrated instead of love, and friendships dissolving because of jealously instead of women being happy for others' blessings.

August 26

Praise Ye the Lord, Praise Ye the Lord, Praise Ye the Lord.
—**Psalm 146:1**

***L*adies,**
I do not need to comment about this verse; it speaks for itself!

August 27

But my God shall supply all your needs according to his riches in glory by Christ Jesus.
—**Philippians 4:19**

***L*adies,**
Focus on the one who can provide!

August 28

Because thou hast been my help, therefore in the shadow of thy wings will I rejoice. My soul follow hard after thee: thy right hand uphold me.
—**Psalm 63:7–8**

***L*adies,**
Your help comes from the Lord.

August 29

And after you have suffered a little while, the God of all grace, who has called you to his eternal glory in Christ, will himself restore, confirm, strengthen and establish you.
—**1 Peter 5:10**

L**adies,**
Your trials are not about you but about God's Glory.

August 30 and 31

The Lord replied, "My presence will go with you, and I will give you rest.
—**Exodus 33:14**

L**adies,**
If you want rest from your weary mind and body, seek God's presence.

SEPTEMBER

Dose of

TRUSTING GOD'S PLANS

September 1

I am the light of the world, whoever follows me will never walk in darkness, but will have the light of life.
—**John 8:12**

L**adies,**
Keep walking with God into your new season. Follow His glorious light, and know that when you encounter fog along the way, keep hold of God's hand and He will move you through. God's light never fades; it only dimmers when we lose faith in Him or let go of His hand. Focus, walk, and hold His hand; His bright sunshine shall lead the way. Be blessed in your new season. Praise God.

September 2

Christ has set us free. He wants us to enjoy freedom. So stand firm. Don't let the chains of slavery hold you again.
—**Galatians 5:1**

L**adies,**
Do not allow the tricks of Satan to keep you in bondage. Jesus is the key to release you from prison.
Prison: alcoholism, gossip, adultery, bitterness, jealousy, abuse, victimhood, unhappiness, denial, lack of self-love, and dependence on man.

September 3

For God is not a God of disorder but of peace as in all the congregations of the Lord's people.
—**1 Corinthians 14:33**

L**adies,**
If your lives are filled with confusion, focus on God. He is the only one who can provide peace of mind during chaos.

September 4

A woman who has friends must herself be friendly, but there is a friend who sticks closer than a sister.
—**Proverbs 18:24**

***L*adies,**
We must be friendly and unselfishly support our sisters. Remember, there is no friend like Jesus. Jesus is a true friend, who reaches for your hand and touches your heart forever.

September 5

To everything there is a season, and a time to every purpose under the heaven.
—**Ecclesiastes 3:1**

***L*adies,**
When God moves you into a new season in your life, trust God. Do not allow others to hold you back in a previous season because they are not ready to move forward. Trusting God will bring new blessings.

September 6

If we confess our sins, he is faithful and just and will forgive us our sins and purify us from all unrighteousness.
—**1 John 1:9**

***L*adies,**
We all have sinned, but we do not have to remain in that season of our lives. Repent and ask God for forgiveness, and all will be forgiven. Do not allow others to continue the blame game. God says it is done; therefore, it is done in Jesus' name. Praise God!

September 7 and 8

Love is Patient and Kind, never jealous, boastful, proud or rude. Love is not selfish or quick tempered. It does not keep a record of wrongs that others do. Love rejoices in the truth, but not in evil. Love is always supportive, loyal, hopeful and trusting. Love never fails!
—**1 Corinthians 13:4**

***L*adies,**
The kind of love in Corinthians is a love that only God can provide. As children of God, our duty is to always think, what would Jesus do in all circumstances? Then and only then will we start to reflect to others the love God gives us daily.

September 9

Therefore you have no excuse, O man, every one of you who judges. For in passing judgment on another you condemn yourself, because you, the judge, practice the very same things.
—**Romans 2:1**

***L*adies,**
Why are you judging her?
Have you not sinned in the past? How did you feel when you were judged? We all make mistakes. No woman is perfect, including you! So, lift up and support your sister as Christ supports you unconditionally!

September 10

That your faith should not stand in the wisdom of men, but in the power of God.
—**1 Corinthians 2:5**

***L*adies,**
Avoid, negate, and remove all those who do not have faith that God can and will handle all your situations! Faithless people are not aware of the power of God.

September 11

Those things which ye have both learned, and received, and heard, and seen in me, do; and the God of Peace shall be with you.
—**Philippians 4:9**

***L*adies,**
Study the word of God. Follow and imitate the teaching and behavior of Jesus in your lives daily and peace shall be present.

September 12

Your word is a lamp to my feet and a light for my path.
—**Psalm 119:105**

***L*adies,**
Allow God to order your steps.

September 13

Jesus saith unto him, I am the way, the truth, and the life, no man cometh unto the Father but by me.
—**John 14:6**

***L*adies,**
Only Jesus can lead you to God. Do not be fooled by earthly men.

September 14 and 15

And let us not grow weary of doing good, for in due season we will reap, if we do not give up.
—**Galatians 6:9**

***L*adies,**
During your waiting period, the Devil will slither his way into your mind and place doubt that God will not give you the blessing you are waiting for. Do not allow Satan's lies to discourage you. Instead, trust and focus on God, not the circumstances around you.

September 16

The faithful love of the Lord never ends! His mercies never cease. Great is his faithfulness; his mercies begin a fresh each morning. I say to myself, "The Lord is my inheritance: therefore, I will hope in him! The Lord is good to those who depend on him. So, it is good to wait quietly for salvation from the Lord.
—**Lamentations 3:22**

***L*adies,**
Faith moves God!

September 17

And He has said to me, "My grace is sufficient for you, for power is perfected in weakness." Most gladly, therefore, I will rather boast about my weakness, so that the power of Christ may dwell in me.
—**2 Corinthians 12:9**

***L*adies,**
Sometimes, while waiting on the Lord, we get stressed out physically and emotionally, but our God said that in our weakness, his power is manifested in us. Praise God!

September 18

For I know the plans I have for you, declares the Lord. Plans to prosper you and not harm you, plans to give you hope and a future.
—**Jeremiah 29:11**

***L*adies,**
Coincidences are not part of God's vocabulary.

September 19

You intended to harm me, but God intended it for good.
—**Genesis 50:20**

***L*adies,**
The Devil thought his plans (doubt, divide, and eventually destroy) would separate us from God. The Devil forgot that God loves us!

September 20

The steps of a good man are ordered by the Lord, And he delights in his way though he fall, he shall not be utterly cast down, for the Lord upholds him with His hand.
—**Psalm 37:23–24**

***L*adies,**
This Lord's steps guarantee protection, provision, and peace!

September 21–22

Be still and know I am God.
—**Psalm 46:10**

Ladies,
Get off the worldly rollercoaster, and be still in the presence of God!
Peace only comes when you sit in the presence of God!

September 23

And the fruit of righteousness is sown in peace of them that make peace.
—**James 3:18**

Ladies,
Are you a peacemaker?

September 24 and 25

For many deceivers are entered into the world, who confess not that Jesus is Christ is come in the flesh. This is a deceiver and an antichrist.
—**2 John 1:7**

Ladies,
Do not be deceived by those who profess being God. Who profess spirituality, energy, and love without professing God the Father and God the Son!
Be aware of Satan's allies; they are everywhere.

September 26

And I will give you a new heart, and a new spirit I will put within you. And I will remove the heart of a stone from your flesh and give you a heart of flesh.
—**Ezekiel 36:26**

Ladies,
Have you ever wondered why you feel compassion for someone who has treated you wrong? Why you are now able to view that person differently? And why if you ever saw an old friend again, who had stopped communicating with you, you would no

longer be upset but forgiving? Because *now* the spirit of God has taken control and softened your heart.

September 27

Every word of God is pure; he is a shield unto them that put their trust in him.
—**Proverbs 30:5**

***L*adies,**
Trust God with all things in your life. He offers you protection and peace.

September 28

The Lord shall guide us continually, and satisfy our soul in drought, and make fat thy bones, and thou shall be like a watered garden, and like a spring of water, whose waters fail not.
—**Isaiah 58:11**

***L*adies,**
When you allow God to direct your path, you will not thirst.

Thirst: fret over finances, family disorder, job pressure, children's peer pressure, and health.

Focusing on God provides peace in our minds, which quenches our thirst.

September 29 and 30

Jesus Christ the same yesterday and today and forever ...
—**Hebrews 13:8**

***L*adies,**
Is there anyone you know who has remained the same?

Anyone?

Anyone who once was a friend, spouse, or cousin you knew would be there until the end? Unfortunately, no earthly person, including ourselves, remains the same. But our almighty God will never change; He will remain with us regardless.

OCTOBER

Dose of

BEING STILL

October 1

And when Jesus saw her he called her to Him and said unto her, woman thou art loosed from thine infirmity. And he laid his hands on her and immediately she was made straight, and glorified God.
—**Luke 13:12–13**

***L*adies,**
God is a healer! Not only does He heal our bodies but also our minds!

Bodies: cancer, stroke, anemia, arthritic pain, infertility, and drug addiction.
Minds: depression, anxiety, fear, mental illness, and bitterness.

Praise and honor to the almighty God for making us whole again in the new season.

October 2

And he said unto her daughter be of good comfort thy Faith has made thee whole go in Peace.
—**Luke 8:48**

***L*adies,**
Faith in God shall lead you to the divine destiny God has for you. Be patient, focus, and wait on God. He has brought you through the ninth month of this year. Do not doubt. He can bring you to the end of this year.

October 3 and 4

Behold I give unto you power to tread on serpents and scorpions, and over all the power of the enemy and nothing shall by any means hurt you.
—**Luke 10:19–20**

***L*adies,**
Fear nothing. The almighty God has you covered by the blood of Jesus. No weapon formed against you can prosper when you are in the will of God!

October 5

Until I come, spend your time reading Scripture out loud to one another. Spend your time preaching and teaching, don't fail to use the gift the Holy Spirit, gave you.
—1 Timothy 4:13–16

***L*adies,**
In order to reach others with the Word, you first must study the Word.

October 6

For we walk by faith, not by sight.
—2 Corinthians 5:7

For I know the plans I have for you, declares the Lord, plans for welfare and not for evil, to give you a future and a hope.
—Jeremiah 29:11

***L*adies,**
God and only God knows your future. Trust Him, take hold of His hand, and allow Him to lead. He gives you so much peace when you depend on Him.

October 7 and 8

He said to her, Daughter, your faith has healed you. Go in peace and be freed from your suffering.
—Mark 5:34

***L*adies,**
Do you have faith that no matter what the doctor says, you are healed?

October 9

Enter God's kingdom through the narrow gate. The gate is large and the road is wide that lead to death and hell. Many people go that way. But the gate is small and the road is narrow that lead to life. Only a few people find it.
—Matthew 7:13–14

***L*adies,**
Seeking God and following His destination for your life is not easy, but it is the only way. On the road, you will experience naysayers, but continue your walk with Christ and peace shall encompass you.

October 10

I am with you. I will watch over you. I will bring you back to this land. I will not leave you until I have done what I have promised you.
—Genesis 28:15

***L*adies,**
Stop and trust that God will place you on the path that He designed for you.

October 11

Jesus had worked a lot of miracles among the people, but they were still not willing to have faith in him.
—John 12:37

***L*adies,**

Family and friends may not accept the journey God has given you. They may talk behind your back or even to your face because you chose to follow God's plans for your life. When your life does not fit into the world's view of how it should look, haters surface with negativity.

October 12 and 13

But the hour cometh, and now is when the true worshippers shall worship the Father in Spirit and in Truth; for the father seeketh such to worship him.
—**John 4:23**

***L*adies,**

Stay focused on pleasing God, not others. When you worship God in spirit and truth, you will receive God's peace.

October 14

Unto thee, O 'Lord, do I lift up my soul.
—**Psalm 25:1**

***L*adies,**

Jesus saved your soul from Satan's wicked hands. Jesus' suffering proves His undying, unconditional love, and He is worthy of daily praise.

October 15

Let us therefore come boldly unto the throne of grace, that we may obtain mercy, and find grace to help in time of need.
—**Hebrews 4:16**

Ladies,
Stop fretting about your lack of money to pay your bills. Trust God and His promised word that He shall supply all your needs when steadfast faith is present.

October 16

Believe in the Lord Jesus. Then you and your family will be saved.
—**Acts 16:31**

Ladies,
Your obedience to God shall cover your family.

October 17

And he said, Come, and when Peter was to come down out of the ship, he walked on the water, to go to Jesus. But when he saw the wind boisterous, he was afraid; and beginning to sink, he cried, saying, Lord save me.
—**Matthew 14:29–30**

Ladies,
When you take your eyes off Jesus, you allow your circumstances to defeat you. When the storms of life are around you, keep your eyes on Him, not on your need for help. Jesus will conquer the storm!

October 18

And the man said, The woman thou gavest to be with me, she gave me of the tree, and I did eat.
—**Genesis 3:12**

Ladies,
If others are blaming you, seek the presence of God and stay focused!

October 19

Even as the Son of man came not to be ministered unto, but to minister, and to give his life a ransom for many.
—**Matthew 20:2**

L**adies,**
Are you serving others according to God's plan?

October 20

The lord shall fight for you, and ye shall hold your peace.
—**Exodus 14:14**

L**adies,**
Be still when the Devil thinks the economy is your resource, when judgmental people want to live in your past, when the doctor brings you bad news, when the bills continue to accumulate, or when family lacks trust in the power of God. Just be still, and put on peripheral-view blinders so you can focus only on God as you move through His divine plan.

October 21 and 22

Trust in the Lord with all thine heart; and lean not unto thine own understanding. In all thy ways acknowledge him, and he shall direct thy paths.
—**Exodus 14:14**

L**adies,** stop seeking earthly people for direction. Seek God, focus on Him, hold onto His right hand, and allow Him to lead you.

October 23

If ye be willing and obedient, ye shall eat the good of the land.
—**Isaiah 1:19**

***L*adies,**
Do you remember as a child when you learned to obey, and when you did not, there were consequences to your disobedience? As a daughter of God, if you follow His will (be obedient), focus on Him, trust Him, depend on Him, and praise and honor Him, you shall inherit all the blessings He has awaiting you.

October 24

I find my rest in God alone, He is the One who saves me.
—**Psalms 62:1**

***L*adies,**
When your life becomes full of uncertainty, trust God and receive His blessing of a peaceful mind.

October 25

Submit yourselves, then to God. Resist the devil, and he will flee from you.
—**James 4:7**

***L*adies,**
Submission to God releases you from the bondage of Satan's world: negativity, depression, bitterness, judgment, and dependence on man.

October 26

There is only one lawgiver and judge, the one who is able to save and destroy. But you, who are to judge your neighbor?
—**James 4:11**

***L*adies,**
Do not judge others, and do not listen to the judgments against you from others. Only God can judge you. God knows your heart, and if what you are doing is sincere, focus and follow God's will and plans for your life. Live in your new season.

October 27

The Lord is not slow in keeping his promise, as some understand slowness, instead he is patient and with you, not wanting anyone to perish, but everyone to come to repentance.
—**2 Peter 3:9**

***L*adies,**
God loves you!
He awaits you to come to Him. God gives you free will to seek Him and for you to allow Him to guide you in this life journey. Do not keep Him waiting; His return is soon.

October 28

Now listen, you who say, Today or tomorrow we will go to this or that city. We will spend a year there, we will buy and sell and make money. You don't even know what will happen tomorrow. What is your life? It is a mist that appears for a little while, then it disappears.
—**James 4:13**

***L*adies,**
Live in the present; tomorrow is not promised. Keep your eyes and mind on Jesus, the mind regulator. He is the shining light in your eyes that never dims.

October 29

And the Peace of God, which passeth all understanding, shall keep your hearts and minds through Christ Jesus.
—**Philippians 4:7**

***L*adies,**
Remaining in the presence of God removes you emotionally from worldly disorder. In fact, the peace of God is so miraculous that nothing or no one can enter the divine hedge of protection that God has placed around you.

October 30

Rejoice in the Lord always and again I say Rejoice.
—**Philippians 4:4**

***L*adies,**
Each day brings a new challenge; however, it does not matter what it is. God will make a way. So do not fret. Instead, praise God for His faithfulness in keeping you from falling prey to negativity.

October 31

I love you Lord
You give me strength, the Lord is my rock and my fort. He is the one who saves me. My God is my rock. I go to him for safety. I call out to the Lord. He is worthy of praise. He saves me from my enemies. The ropes of death were almost wrapped around me. He reached down from heaven. He took hold of me, he lifted me out of

deep waters. He saved me from my powerful enemies. He set me free from those who were too strong for me.
—**Psalms 18:1–4, 16–17**

***L*adies,**

Did God save you from a situation and place you on His divine road of purpose and praise for Him? If so, praise God from this day forward, and testify of His faithfulness.

NOVEMBER

Dose of

GOD'S FAITHFULNESS

November 1

The Lord will command his angels to take good care of you. They will lift you up in their hands. Then you won't trip over a stone. You will walk all over lions and cobras. You will crush mighty lions and poisonous snakes. The Lord says, "I will save the one who loves me." I will keep him safe because he trusts in me. He will call out to me, and I will answer him. I will be with him in times of trouble. I will save him.
—**Psalm 91:11–16**

***L*adies,**
Has God not taken care of you this entire year? Then do not fret about anything that may be attempting to challenge your faith in God. Give all circumstances to God; He shall defeat your worries. Focus, stand, and then bow at the presence of God. This is the eleventh month, and you are still here by the grace, mercy, and unconditional love of God.

November 2

The Lord and King is the Holy One of Israel. He says, "You will find peace and rest when you turn away from your sins and depend on me. You will receive the strength you need when you stay calm and trust in me.
—**Isaiah 30:15**

Always give thanks to God the Father for everything. Give thanks to him in the name of our Lord Jesus Christ.
—**Ephesians 5:20**

***L*adies,**
Do not condemn yourselves for feeling needy. Instead, in the comfort of our Savior, find your strength in His loving presence. Thank Him for always being there!

November 3

Peacemakers who sow in peace reap harvest of righteousness.
—**James 3:18**

L**adies**
When you consume yourself with peace, which is only found in the presence of God, the circumstances of this world are just a mere thought.

November 4

The Lord gives strength to his people; the Lord blesses his people with Peace.
—**Psalm 29:11**

L**adies,**
When you are feeling weary, go to the throne to refuel your spirit for strength to move forward into God's plan for your day.

November 5

For he will command his angels, to guard you in all ways.
—**Psalm 91:11**

L**adies,**
Angels are protectors from God to protect you while you are on this earth. Fear no evil. Trust that God only provides the best protection for you at all times.

November 6

But my God shall supply all your needs according to his riches in glory by Christ Jesus.
—**Philippians 4:19**

***L*adies,**
Do not get caught by the circumstances of this world. God promised He shall supply all of our needs. Our job is to trust!

November 7

Do not merely look out for your own personal interests, but also for the interest of others.
—**Philippians 2:4**

***L*adies,**
Love your fellow woman.

November 8

Christ did not send me to baptize. He sent me to preach the good news. He commanded me not to use the kind of wisdom that people commonly use. That would take all the power away from the cross of Christ.
—**1 Corinthians 1:17**

***L*adies,**
When you minister to another sister, do not worry about how you sound or if you are Scripture savvy. Testify on God's faithfulness. A true, joyful spirit will soften the hardness of any willing heart!

November 9

He said, "Father, if you are willing, take this cup of suffering from me. But do what you want, not what I want." An angel from heaven appeared to Jesus and gave him strength.
—**Luke 22:42**

***L*adies,**
Sometimes following God's will for your life is difficult, but if you ask God for strength, He shall provide you with unbelievable strength to maneuver through any situation. But you must ask and then trust.
Even Jesus received strength from God because of the cross journey He knew He was about to endure, not for His sake but for ours. Praise His holy name for His unconditional love.

November 10

For if any be a hearer of the word, and not a doer, he is like unto a man be holding his natural face in a glass.
—**James 1:23**

We all, with unveiled faces, are reflecting the Glory of the Lord and are being transformed into the same image from glory to glory; this is from the Lord who is the Spirit.
—**2 Corinthians 3:18**

***L*adies,**
When you look at yourselves in the mirror, do you see characteristics of Jesus? When you make yourselves present to the world, others should see God in you. The only way for this transformation to take place is by your willingness to get close to God through His word. When you are interested in someone or something, you spend all your time trying to know him or work overtime to purchase that something you want.
Then isn't God, the only one who has sustained you, more worthy? Study God's word daily so everyone can see God in you.

November 11 and 12

Trust in the Lord will all your heart, and lean not on your own understanding, in all your ways acknowledge him, and he shall direct your paths.
—**Proverbs 3:5–6**

***L*adies,**
Trusting God is looking through the eyes of the Lord. Our vision likes to project on tomorrow. But God said to not worry about tomorrow and to focus on Him.

November 13

But they that wait upon the Lord shall renew their strength; they shall mount up with wings as eagles. They shall run, and not be weary. And they shall walk and not faint.
—**Isaiah 40:31**

***L*adies,**
Are you waiting on God? Trust it will happen.

November 14

Why do you call me Lord, and still don't do what I say? Some people come to me and do what I say. I will show you what they are like. They are like someone who builds a house. He digs down deep and sets it on solid rock. When a flood comes, the river rushes against the house. But the water can't shake it. The house is well built. But here is what happens when people listen to my words and do not obey them. They are like someone who builds a house on soft ground instead of solid rock. The moment the river rushes against the house, it falls down. It is completely destroyed.
—**Luke 6:46–49**

***L*adies,**
In order to reap the blessings of our Father, you must trust His whispers and obey. No matter how impossible it appears, trust God.

November 15 and 17

The earth is the Lord's and the fullness thereof; the world, and they that dwell therein. For he hath founded it upon the seas and established it upon the floods. Who shall ascend into the hill of the Lord? He hath clean hands, and a pure heart; who hath not lifted up his soul unto vanity, nor sworn deceitfully. He shall receive the blessing from the Lord, and righteousness from the God of his salvation. This is the generation of them that seek him that seek thy face, O Jacob. Selah. Lift up your heads, O ye gates; and be ye lift up ye everlasting doors; and the King of Glory shall come in. Who is this King of glory? The Lord strong and mighty the Lord mighty in battle. Lift up your heads, O ye gates; even lift them up, ye everlasting doors; and the King of Glory shall come in. Who is this King of Glory? The Lord of hosts, he is the King of Glory, Selah.
—**Psalm 24:1–10**

***L*adies,**
God is mighty and can defeat any storm in your life. But you must trust that He can. Negative circumstances that are currently present are tricks of the Devil to plant a seed of doubt in your mind. Trust God, and follow His will for your life. God never fails those who depend on Him.

November 18 and 19

He got up and ordered the wind and the huge waves to stop. The storm quieted down, it was completely calm.
—**Luke 8:23–25**

***L*adies,**
There are many different storms in your life: financial, health, or job loss. Sometimes, God allows storms to get our attention so we can truly have faith in Him and His ability, which results in true dependency on Him.

November 20

The Lord said to Joshua, "Get up" what are you doing down there on your face? Israel has sinned, I made a covenant with them. I commanded them to keep it. But they have broken it. They have taken some of the things that had been set apart to me in a special way to be destroyed. They have stolen. They have lied. They have taken the things they stole and have put them with their own things. That is why the men of Israel can't stand up against their enemies. They turn their backs and run. It is because I have decided to let them be destroyed. You must destroy the things you took that had been set apart to me. If you do not, I will not be with you anymore.
—**Joshua 7:10–12**

***L*adies,**
Does chaos consume your life all the time? If so, you need to reexamine why. Sometimes the chaos may be due to the sin in your life. In order for it to change, it first must be revealed. No, you do not have to confess to others or even to this world, but you have to be honest with yourself and, most importantly, repent to God.

November 21 and 22

For the Lord your God is God of gods and Lord of lords, the great, the mighty and the awesome God who is not partial and takes no bribe.
—**Deuteronomy 10:17**

***L*adies,**
God is awesome and is to be praised always.

November 23

Give Thanks in all circumstances, for this is God's will for you in Christ Jesus.
—**1 Thessalonians 5:18**

***L*adies,**
Praise God for his continual faithfulness in your life. Be thankful that you have the undying, unconditional love of God no matter what.

November 24

Cast thy burden upon the Lord, and he shall Sustain thee; he shall Never suffer the righteous to be moved.
—**Psalm 55:22**

***L*adies,**
Trust in God. He can and will keep you during difficult times. Trust Him. Those who belittled, abandoned, blamed, and ignored you shall be only a mere thought, because God will intervene and delete all painful experiences so He can use you to do His will. God does not break a promise. God is the ultimate friend.
There's nobody like God.

November 25

And, behold, I am with thee, and will keep thee in all places whither thou goest, and will bring thee again into this land; for I will not leave thee, until I have done that which I have spoken to thee of.
—**Genesis 28:15**

***L*adies,**
God is with you in spirit. God sends His angels to watch over you. Fear not. God is always present in your life, even when there is no earthly being present. God is there.

November 26

The Lord gives his people strength, The Lord blesses them with Peace.
—**Psalm 29:11**

***L*adies,**
When you rely on Jesus, you will encounter peaceful days.

November 27

People who don't take care of their relatives, and especially their own families, have given up their faith. They are worse than someone who doesn't have faith in the Lord.
—1 Timothy 5:8

***L*adies,**
Your family is a gift from God. Remember to love, cherish, and support them.

November 28

Praise the Lord. Give thanks to the Lord, for he is good, his love Endures Forever.
—Psalm 106:1

***L*adies,**
Thank God for sending His Son to save our souls! Praise God for His unconditional love.

November 29

He has delivered us from the domain of darkness and transferred us to the kingdom of his beloved Son, in whom we have redemption, the forgiveness of sins.
—Colossians 1:13–14

***L*adies,**
Praise God for delivering us!

November 30

But I will sacrifice a Thank offering to you. I will sing a song of thanks. I will do what I have promised. Lord, you are the one who saves me.
—**Jonah 2:9**

***L*adies,**
Reflect back over the past eleven months. Has God kept you despite your circumstances, despite your doubt, and despite yourself? Yes, He has! Shout God's goodness and faithfulness to all.

DECEMBER

Dose of

GOD'S LOVE

December 1

For God so loved the world, that he gave his only begotten son, that whosoever believe in Him should not perish, but have everlasting life.
—**John 3:16**

***L*adies,**
God loves you.

December 2

And the angel came in unto her, and said, Hail, thou that art highly favored, the Lord is with thee; blessed art thou among women.
—**Luke 1:28**

***L*adies,**
Do you know that you are favored by God? Stop allowing others to demean you, and stop doubting your ability to stand against life's challenges.

All you need is to trust and depend on God. You are a daughter of the almighty God! You are a rare, precious gem—an original. Stand up and view yourself like the princess that you are. Your Father God loves you. Even Mary had doubt when the angel told her she would bring forth the Son of God. "How shall this be, seeing I know not a man?" (Luke 1:34). She soon realized that nothing is impossible with God.

December 3

Mary said, "My soul gives glory to The Lord. My spirit delights in God my Savior. He has taken note of me even though I am not important. From now on all people will call me blessed. The Mighty One has done great things for me. His name is Holy."
—**Luke 1:46–49**

***L*adies,**
Recognize how favored you are. It is December, and you are still in your right mind! God has kept you.

December 4

Behold, God is mine helper; The Lord is with them that uphold my soul. He shall reward evil unto mine enemies; cut them off in thy truth. I will freely sacrifice unto thee: I will praise thy name, O Lord; for it is good. For he hath delivered me out of all trouble; and mine hath seen his desire upon mine enemies.
—Psalm 54:4–7

***L*adies,**
God is a deliverer, provider, and protector; fret not any worldly circumstance. God shall sustain!

December 5

I am sure that the One who began a good work in you will carry it on until it is completed, that will be on the day Christ Jesus returns.
—1:6 Philippians

***L*adies,**
Joy is not circumstantial. Joy is based upon Jesus. In the midst of life's difficult circumstances, you can rejoice because God has secured your future while sustaining your present (excerpt from a sermon of Pastor Charlie Dates).

December 6

Thou wilt keep her in perfect peace, whose mind is stayed on thee. Trust ye in the Lord forever; for in the Lord Jehovah is everlasting strength.
—Isaiah 26:3–4

***L*adies,**
When you begin to feel weary or begin to worry, pray to the almighty God to strengthen you to sustain.

December 7

And she shall bring forth a son, and thou shall call his name Jesus. For He shall save his people from their sins.
—**<u>Matthew 1:21</u>**

***L*adies,**
You are not the savior. Only Jesus is.
Stop trying to save others—friends, spouses, children, and family members. You are blocking the works of God. Testify, speak, and praise his name to others about what he has done for you, but you cannot save anyone. Do not be a rescuer! Pray that others will seek Jesus.

December 8

And Joseph also went up from Galilee, out of the city of Nazareth, into Judea, unto the city of David, which is called Bethlehem; To be taxed with Mary his espoused wife, being great with child.
—**<u>Luke 2:45</u>**

***L*adies,**
Joseph obeyed the will of God and took Mary as his wife, regardless of what others thought.
Follow God's will for your life, regardless of what others say or think. God is the only judge.

December 9 and 10

Be still and know that. I am God!
—**Psalm 46:10**

***L*adies,**
When life circumstances are out of control, when uncertainty hovers, and when situations appear bleak, remember to focus on the almighty way maker, God. He shall embrace you with His peace.

December 11

The Lord shall fight for you, and ye shall hold your peace.
—**Exodus 14:14**

***L*adies,**
No need to fret about those who despise you; your almighty God will protect you. Continue to move into the upcoming year.

December 12 and 13

Mary asked the angel, How can this happen? I am a virgin?
—**Luke 1:34**

***L*adies,**
Sometimes God tests our faith in Him by requesting what appears impossible. However, remember that God never fails. God can do all things.

December 14 and 16

The angel answered, The Holy Spirit will come down to you, and God's power will come over you!
—**Luke 1:35**

***L*adies,**
When God requests something from you, fear not and walk in faith. God will give you all you need to complete the assignment.

December 17 and 18

For with God Nothing is impossible.
—**Luke 1:37**

***L*adies,**
If you cannot see a way out of whatever is happening in your life at this moment, focus on God. He is the way, and nothing is impossible for Him to handle. Believe.

December 19

And Blessed is she that believe: for there shall be a performance of those things which were told her from the Lord.
—**Luke 1:45**

***L*adies,**
Why is it so hard for you to believe God's promise to make a way? (Philippians 4:19: "but my God shall supply all my needs.")

December 20 and 21

He has saved us from our enemies. We are rescued from all who hate us. All of that will happen because our God is tender and caring. His kindness will bring the rising sun to us from heaven. It will shine on those living in darkness an in the shadow of death. It will guide our feet on the path of peace.
—**Luke 1:71, 74, 78**

***L*adies,**
Jesus is the only reason we celebrate this season. His birth was the only way to salvation. Does your heart reflect love, the true meaning of Christmas? That is the meaning of Jesus' birth—love.

December 22 and 23

Joseph woke up. He did what the angel of the Lord commanded him to do. He took Mary home as his wife.
—**Matthew 1:24**

***L*adies,**
Obedience is the key in this verse. When God asks you to do something, no matter what, follow Him.

December 24

I Jesus have sent mine angel to testify unto you these things in the churches. I am the root and the offspring of David and the bright and morning star.
—**Revelation 22:16**

***L*adies,**
This Christmas, follow the light of Christ our Savior and peace shall surround you.

December 25

And the Angel said unto them, fear not; for behold, I bring you good tidings of great joy, which shall be to all people. For unto you is born this day in the city of David a Savior which is Christ The Lord. And this shall be a sign unto you; Ye shall find the babe wrapped in swaddling clothes, lying in a manager. And suddenly there was with the angel a multitude of the heavenly host praising God, and saying, Glory to God in the highest, and on earth peace, Good will toward men.
—**Luke 2:10:14**

***L*adies,**
Our Savior, Christ the Lord, is born! Let's rejoice and sing praises to God for Jesus.

December 26

But I will trust in your faithful love. My heart is filled with joy because you will save me. I will sing to the Lord. He has been so good to me.
—**Psalm 13:5–6**

***L*adies,**
Jesus saves! You are loved and have everlasting life because of our Savior, who was born, died, and was resurrected.

December 27

The grace of our Lord God Jesus Christ be with you all. Amen.
—**2 Thessalonians 3:18**

***L*adies,**
Grace is God's favor, God's good will. God only wants the best for you. Praise Him; there is no other love like this.

December 28 and 29

But I Trust in your unfailing love, my heart rejoices in your salvation. I will sing the Lord Praise! For he has been good to me!
—**Psalm 13:5–6**

***L*adies,**
Reflect on this ending year. Has God's unfailing, unconditional love sustained you when you thought you could not make it another day? When you could not see your way out of a situation?

December 30

For God so loved the world that he gave his one and only son, that whoever believes in him shall not perish but have eternal life.
—**John 3:16**

***L*adies,**
"Have you sacrificed? Giving up something that no longer worked in order to stay close to the sacred" (Mark Nepo).

God sacrificed His son to come down into this wicked world to save you and me. What a love.

December 31

I desire to do your will, my God; your law is within my heart.
—**Psalm 40:8**

***L*adies,**
This year, have you followed the will of God for your life?
How would you know?
You would know if your heart is different from January of this year.

Seeking total dependence on God, loving others more, and forgiving those who wronged you are results from a life intertwined with the presence of God.

Epilogue

A new season—I am out of the old and into the new door that God has opened for me:

Priscilla, who depended on earthly things/man. **Done!**

Priscilla, who cared what others thought of her. **Done!**

Priscilla, who allowed Satan to detour her off her God-given path. **Done!**

Priscilla, who enabled others instead of leading them to Christ. **Done!**

My heart is so hidden in God that a man has to seek Him first just to find it (paraphrased from Max Lucado).

The Lord is Holy and Kind. My God is full of tender love. The Lord takes care of those who are as helpless as children. When I was in Great Need he saved Me! I said to myself, "Be calm."

The Lord has been Good to Me. Lord, you have saved me from death. You have dried the tears from my eyes. You have kept me from tripping and falling. So, Now I can enjoy life here with you while I am still living. I will bring an offering of wine to the Lord and thank Him for saving me. I will worship him In front of all his people. —Psalm 116:5–9, 13–14

Dependence is not hindrance if it's on God.